SIMPLE, NON-TECHNICAL

MORE PARS!

SHORT GAME TIPS
+ OFF THE FAIRWAY

from best-selling golf author
CHRISTINA RICCI

WELCOME 10
message from Christina

HOW TO USE 17
the purpose and how to use this book

GAME RESOURCES
where to get help

Find a Golf Professional 22
Golf Lingo 24

GAME ESSENTIALS
how to improve

Mistakes Are Good! 26
Your First Steps 28

FAQs 33
popular questions

No Dumb Questions 34
Equipment & Gear 36
Rules & Etiquette 48
Pace of Play 50
Locker Room Stretch 54
At the Gym 62
Nutrition Tips 64
Practice Time 68
Top 5 Performance Tips 70

LONG GAME

SWING ESSENTIALS 79
start here

An Awesome Grip 81
Understanding Posture 96
Posture on a Plane 101
Posture Setup Keys 114
Alignment 120
Club Setups 128

let's take flight!

LET'S SWING! 157
step-by-step swing progressions

What is Swing Plane?	158
Takeaway Keys	162
Backswing Culprits	172
Structure Begins Here	176
At the Range	182
Rotation vs. Sway	198
On the Course	204

LET'S TEE OFF 213
launch this puppy

Target & Routine	214
Alignment Process	219
Fear of Water	222
Tee Heights	224
Driver Setup Keys	226
Driver Swing Keys	228

FAIRWAY ESSENTIALS 235
let's get airborne

Divots	236
The Swing Arc	240
Help Factor	242
Simplify Impact	248
Steps to Great Impact	254
Swing Plane	264
Swing Keys	266
Practice Pressure	276
Practice Low Point	278
Woods	280

SHORT GAME

BUNKER GAME 287
splash with confidence

What is Bounce?	288
Square vs. Open	290
Bunker Alignment	293
Basic Bunker Shot	294
How Much Sand?	300
Long Greenside	302
Downslope	306
Upslope	308
Firm Sand or Buried Lie	310
Close to the Edge	314
Fairway Bunker	317

CHIPS & PITCHES 323
the essentials

Chip vs. Pitch	325
Capital Y Chips	330
Which Club?	337
Landing Spot	340
Dense Rough	342
Low Runner	344

Uh-oh! Did you order that fried egg?

Reading the Green

If you poured a bucket of water, which way would it flow?

ON THE GREEN   347
take a vacation

Vacation Zone	348
Equipment	352
Lie Angle	356
Reading the Green	358
Alignment	360
Putting Grip	362
Solid Setup	366
Solid Stroke	368
Speed Control	370
Stroke Culprits	375
Groove Tempo	385
Aim vs. Apex	387
Groove Short Putts	388
Long & Downhill	390
Practice Strokes	393
NEXT STEPS	394

WELCOME MESSAGE FROM
Christina Ricci

Welcome to golf! This game is awesome.

It is even more awesome with:
- Fitted equipment
- Professional golf instruction
- Practice (home, range or course)
- Golf fitness & mobility
- Basic knowledge of the rules & etiquette
- A positive attitude

I began my golf journey in 2000. At the time, I lived in Miami and had a marketing business. Being self-employed afforded me the time to dedicate to my golf game. I soon realized that my passion was golf, so I married my two passions: marketing and golf. The result was my first book. *A Girl's On-Course Survival Guide to Golf.* It was marketed to women and I published it as an amateur. It was my journey from a new golfer to a 5-handicap in five years. After the launch of my More Pars YouTube channel, my market opened up to all players.

Amateur to Professional

After many requests for in-person lessons, I decided to take the plunge and get certified as a golf professional.

Many years later, I am now a PGA and LPGA Class A Member, Titleist Performance Institute (TPI): Golf Level 3, Power Level 2 & Fitness Level 2 Coach, as well as a Level Two Crossfit Trainer. With the knowledge of a fitness trainer, I can better train my students for golf.

Body/Swing Connection

I am firm believer in the body/swing connection. Our bodies are the most important factor to effortless golf. Knowing what your body can and cannot do is really the first step to great golf. For example, if your current instructor is asking you to perform a certain position and you cannot physically do it, then it becomes a frustrating experience—for you and the instructor. It's important to train your body for golf. The

golf swing takes under two seconds. It requires super fast muscle firing to achieve speed off the clubface. Focus first on mobility, followed by strength, and then speed.

Get Fitted!
Followed by the body, equipment is the next very important variable to enjoyable golf. I am still amazed when I meet female students for the first time and they pull out steel shafted clubs handed down by their husbands! (Seriously, husbands: Stop This, ha ha!) Your intentions are awesome, but you are not benefitting your wife. Get her properly fitted, so she will have the best chance for success. And same goes for you!

Golf is a demanding sport that requires every bit of you, physically and mentally. To be great at this game, train for both. Invest in lessons, a fitness trainer and read books on the mental game. I offer a comprehensive online resource for golf and golf fitness at morepars..com.

Perseverance, Patience and Practice
The three Ps are the foundation of golf. There are many games within golf and there is no shot that is ever the same. This game requires all three Ps to optimize lasting enjoyment. And always remember that golf is just a game. Don't take yourself too seriously. Seriously! I tried this and it doesn't work. The other

thing that I tried over and over again was looking for the short cuts. There are no shortcuts with the exception of finding a golf professional that speaks your language. That truly is the best short cut to effortless golf.

More Pars Camps!

My More Pars Camps provide the opportunity to personally tailor my instruction for all skill levels. My camps are open to men and women. They are typically limited to small class sizes of six for lots of personal attention. I host across the country at great clubs and resorts, adding locations all the time. I cover all aspects of the game from sinking more putts to better ball striking. Plus, we head out on the course for on-course coaching.

Please visit:
christinariccigolf.com for my current camp schedule.

Golf is a journey.
Let's journey together!

The Purpose of This Book and How to Use It

This book is designed for newer golfers (and a fantastic refresher for avid players). With its portable size it can be used on-course and off-the-course. The focus of this book is to give you an easy step-by-step process to learn the swing and various shots that you'll encounter during a round of golf from tee to green. I provide simple cues and relatable feels that you can incorporate right away. Plus, I answer popular new golfer questions.

NO

common culprits

Clear visuals for more pars.

VISUALLY SPEAKING

When it comes to golf, seeing is believing. My signature cover-to-cover visuals, with easy-to-follow steps and YES/NO tips, make this a learning friendly experience. Plus, this book is a perfect complement to your golf lessons. What? You don't take lessons? Uh-oh! Head to the Game Resources section to find a local Golf Professional.

The YES/NO feature is a Christina signature.

HOW TO USE THIS BOOK
Suggested Steps

Golf is a journey and an ongoing learning process. The game is played best with a strategy from tee to green and in between. There is no cookie-cutter process. Everyone will craft their own game plan to make more pars. I can help you begin (or continue) your journey. The key to success is to focus on one thing at a time. If you try to think of every aspect, you'll drive yourself insane. Instead, create clarity for your game.

HELPFUL ICON TIPS

DO THIS **KEY POINT**

MENTAL

VIDEO

STEP 1
Start with Your First Steps presented on the following pages.

STEP 2
Focus much of your time with setups, posture and swing progressions.

STEP 3
Take action. Get help and practice. Practice can be at home, in your mind, at the range, gym, golf course...get creative!

I invite you to visit MorePars.com to explore videos and all of my online learning resources.

Find a Golf Professional

The PGA of America is made up of nearly 29,000 PGA Professionals who are ready to help you further your love for the game of golf. The PGA of America is here to help you make the most of your golf journey. We seek to establish a fundamental relationship with every golfer, and build on that relationship to give you the resources you need to help you achieve your goals.

HTTPS://WWW.PGA.COM

The LPGA boasts the largest membership of women golf professionals in the world. The LPGA has earned a reputation as the leader in research-based golf education.

HTTPS://PROFESSIONALS.LPGA.COM/FIND-A-TEACHER/FIND

TPI is the world's leading educational organization dedicated to the study of how the human body functions in relation to the golf swing.

HTTPS://WWW.MYTPI.COM/EXPERT

Golf Lingo

Golf has its own language. If you are new to the game or even an experienced player, it is good to be crystal clear on all golf lingo. The following list is specific to swing technique—terms that I reference throughout this book. Use the PGA link to access a comprehensive golf dictionary. You can look up these terms there. Plus, take a look at the ramshill.com link. It covers terms even an avid golfer may not have heard of, such as Barkies, Jungle, and Nip. If there is a term that you are not clear about, reach out to me!

BALL FLIGHTS & CONTACT
Blades/Thin
Blocks
Chunks/Fat
Pushes
Pulls
Slices
Square, Open, Closed

BODY POSITIONS
Chicken Wing
Flaring Trail Elbow
Flat Footed
Flat Shoulder
Hand Depth
Hip Depth
Too Flat
Too Upright
Wrist Flexion/Extension

SWING ARC
Face to Path
Shallow
Steep
Swing Direction
Swing Plane

SWING CULPRITS
Disconnected
Over the Top
Underneath the Plane
Early Extension
Early Release
Sways and Slides
Chicken Wing
Hold On
Flippy or Cupped
Loss of Posture
Torso Hang Back
Swing Positions
Address
Impact
Finish
Follow-Through
Lead Arm Parallel
Pre-Delivery
Takeaway
Transition

KEY PRINCIPLES
Angle of Attack
Ball Speed
Forward Shaft Lean
Launch
Loft
Low Point
Pressure
Sequence
Spin
Swing Speed
Swing Match-ups
Tilts & Bends

HTTPS://WWW.PGA.COM/STORY/GOLF-DICTIONARY-GLOSSARY-GOLF-TERMS

HTTPS://WWW.RAMSHILL.COM/2019/07/25/YOUR-GOLF-SLANG-CHEAT-SHEET

HOW WE LEARN
Mistakes Are Good!

Think back to a time when you learned a new skill, such as driving a car, riding a bicycle, or reading a book. When you first learned this skill, performing it was an active process in which you analyzed and were consciously aware of every movement. Part of this analytical process also meant that you thought carefully about why you were doing what you were doing, to understand how these individual steps fit together. As your ability improved, performing the skill stopped being so conscious, instead becoming more intuitive. It is the same deal with the golf swing!

MISTAKES ARE GOOD
Regardless of skill level, when a new skill set is presented, mistakes and errors are expected. This is how the brain learns to identify what is correct and not correct. As you continue to refine the good from the bad, that is when the movement becomes second-nature. Being able to perform automatically spells learning success and more pars!

GAME ESSENTIALS
Your First Steps

The first step is to ask yourself the important questions:

Why do you play?
Many players enjoy the:
- Outdoors with Nature
- Camaraderie
- Social Component
- Competition
- Business Angle

There is no wrong answer. The key is to identify why you play so you can craft a realistic game plan for improvement.

What are your goals?
Goals are a great place to start crafting a game plan. As a newer golfer, setting realistic and measurable goals creates lots of confidence.

How good do you want to be?
The answer to this question will guide the amount of practice required to improve your game, as well as the number of lessons with a golf professional. There are many facets to this game. Investing in a series of lessons will make the learning process much more enjoyable.

Join a league for newer golfers. It's a great way to meet new pals.

Everyone needs lessons

Only 15 percent of the golfing population invest in professional golf instruction. That blows my mind! Golf is one of the most challenging games on the planet. It's not like riding a bike.

Misdiagnoses

The biggest concern is misdiagnosing your swing faults, which can send you down the wrong road and inhibit your learning. YouTube, Instagram and the like are great. However, nothing beats working one-on-one or in a group setting with a professional instructor.

When I was learning, I visited my pro once or twice a week.

31

Notes

FAQs POPULAR QUESTIONS

NO DUMB
Questions

As a newer golfer, you probably have a lot of questions. Building confidence in your game begins with getting those questions answered. When I was learning the game, my instructor always told me, ***There are no dumb questions. The only dumb question is the one that you don't ask.***

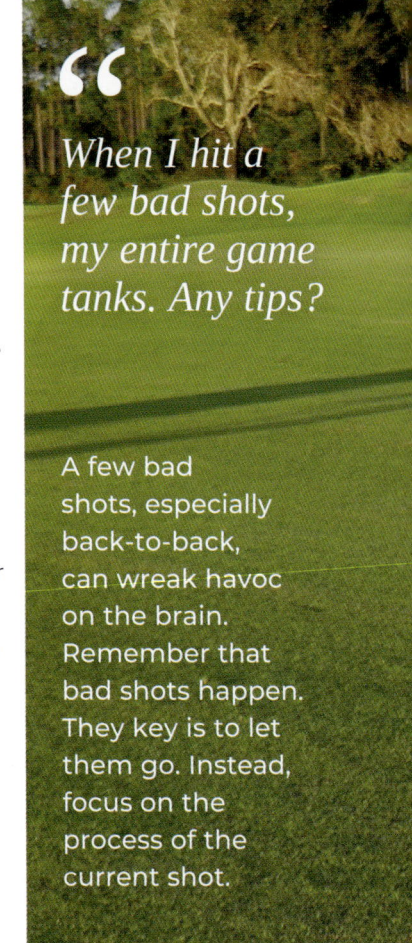

"

When I hit a few bad shots, my entire game tanks. Any tips?

A few bad shots, especially back-to-back, can wreak havoc on the brain. Remember that bad shots happen. They key is to let them go. Instead, focus on the process of the current shot.

35

Equipment & Gear

- Towel
- Ball Marker
- Notepad/Pen:

Take notes at the range or after lessons to keep your swing keys top-of-mind. If you are having a banner day, write down the feels, so you can call on this during a future round.

- Clean Gloves
- Club Brush
- Tees
- Sunblock
- Range Finder
- Golf Balls
- Extra Spikes
- Band Aids
- A More Pars Cap
- Christina's Books and Pocket Guides

> *What do I need for gear?*

Uh-oh! Don't let this happen to you! Pack extra spikes in your golf bag.

Worn or missing spikes

Spikes help to grip the ground so you can leverage it to generate lots of clubhead speed.

> *Should I wait to get fitted?*

If you have, at a minimum, a somewhat repeatable swing, you can be custom fit for clubs, including a putter. Many times people think they have to be a "good" player to get custom fit clubs. Actually, it's the opposite—don't wait because you will play better with custom-fit clubs. A highly-skilled player can compensate for poorly fitted equipment better than a lesser-skilled player. In fact, it may be the equipment that is holding you back from reaching your potential. Many players see significant improvement in their game with new equipment or adjustments to their existing clubs.

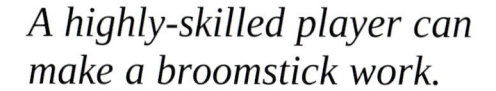

A highly-skilled player can make a broomstick work.

" *What is the difference between wedges?*

There are several differences between wedges. The standard W is typically 44°-48° degrees loft and travels the furthest. Gap wedges (G) range from 50°-52°, sand wedges (S) from 54°-56°, and lob wedges (L) from 58°-64°. It is important to have the right collection of wedges in your bag to provide the best choices for your game.

PXG Wedges

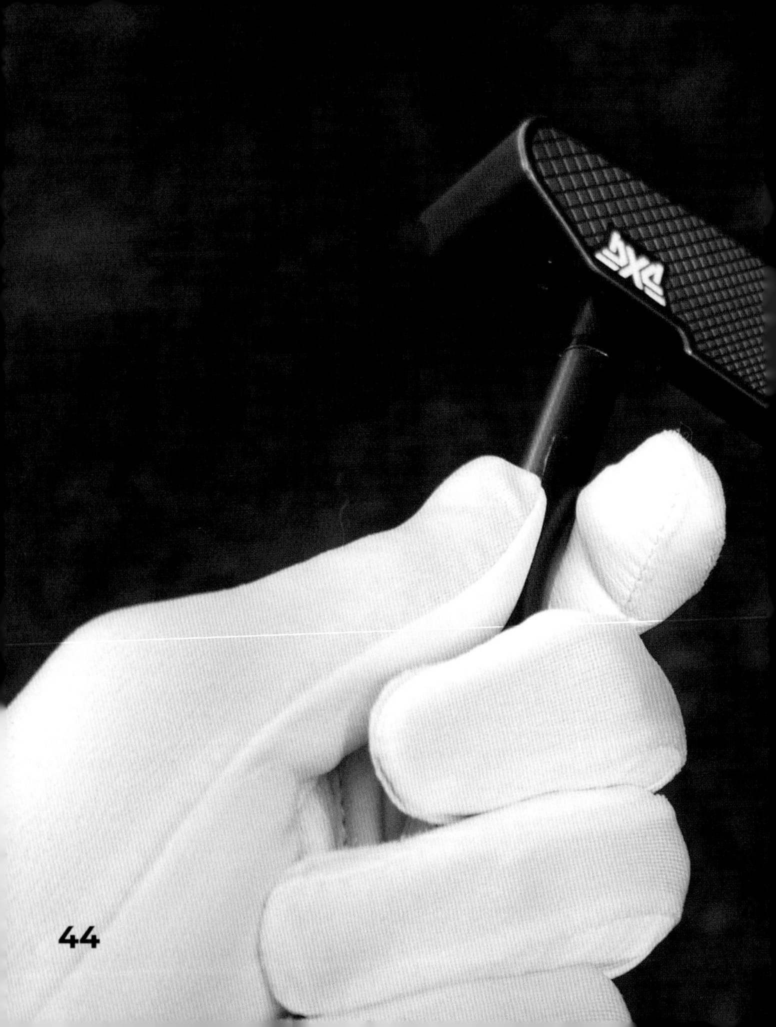

> *Should I wear a glove on the green?*

You rarely see a touring pro wear a glove on the green. The glove is designed to provide control of a club that is moving upwards of 100 mph. On the green, it's all about feel (the many nerve endings in your fingers and hands). The glove can interfere with this feel.

Golf Balls

What ball is right for you?

As a newer player or high-handicapper, your primary concern may be hitting the ball long and straight. Try a low-spin distance ball, which are designed to reduce the side-spin that creates excessive curvature of the ball (slices and hooks). For slower swing speeds, look for brands that offer soft-feel or low compression.

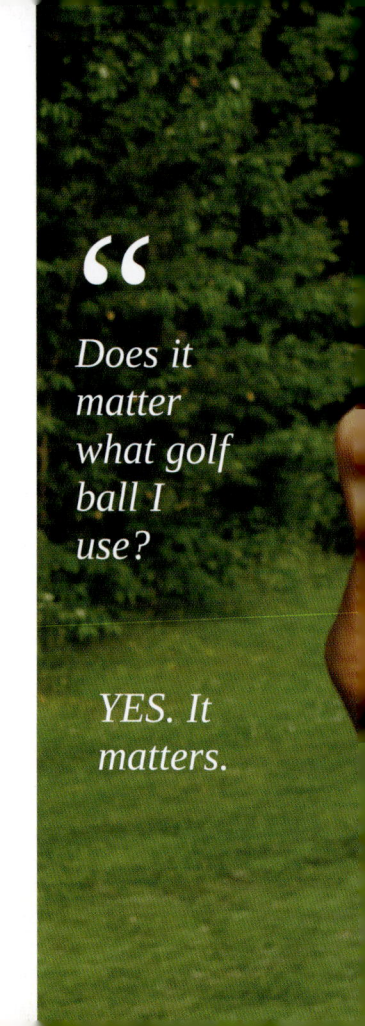

> *Does it matter what golf ball I use?*
>
> YES. It matters.

47

Rules & Etiquette

" *Do I need to know all the rules?*

Absolutely not. If you encounter a rules situation on the course, reference Christina's Golf Rules pocket guide or head to USGA.com.

Never walk in another player's line. This is the golden rule of etiquette.

Committing breaches in etiquette can brand you as a lightweight (and are embarrassing to boot). Head to MissPar.com to get the Golf Etiquette booklet, which includes Golf Lingo.

49

Oh I love her outfit

Oh, no, I think I forgot to turn off the coffee maker!

Should I go with Driver.... or my 3-wood?

> " *I want to play, but what if I hold others up?*

Playing golf with others, especially strangers, can be intimidating for newer players.

50 Pace of Play

To alleviate this stress, focus on the shot at hand with one strong swing feel and positive intentions, such as to get your ball to the target. This will keep your mind occupied.

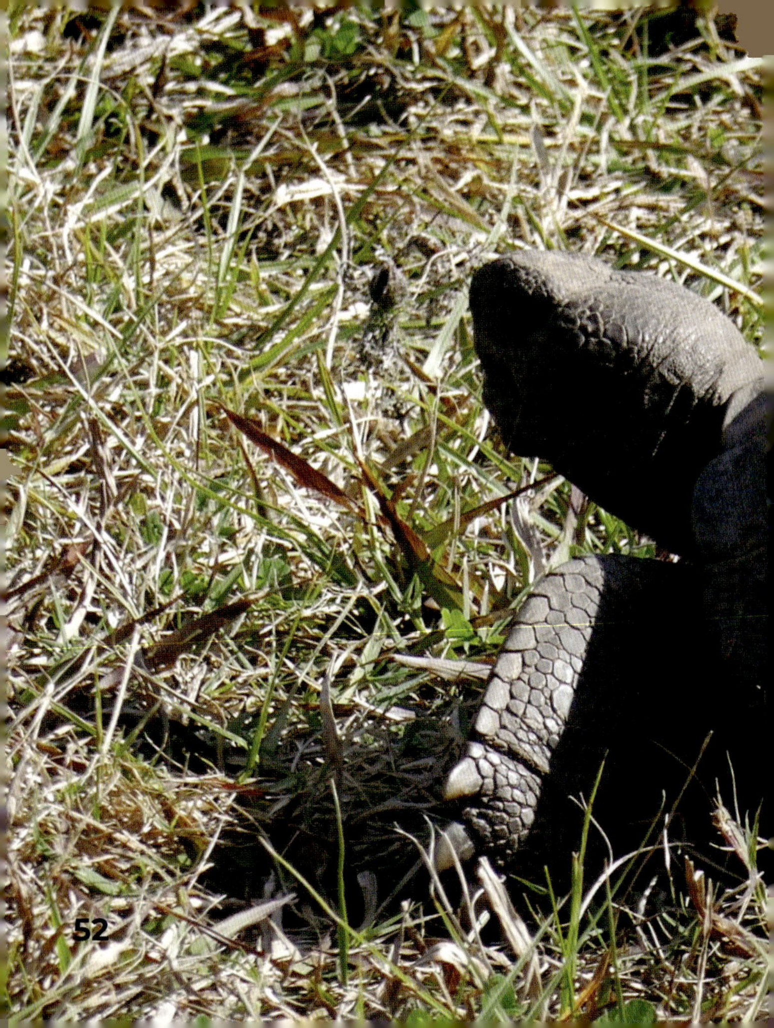

> *Should I pick up mid-hole if I'm really struggling?*

It depends. If you are playing with better players, sometimes it is okay to pick up to keep pace of play. For example, if you are playing a Par 4 and hitting your third shot from the fairway, consider picking up. Announce to the group, then drop up near the green.

Locker Room Stretch

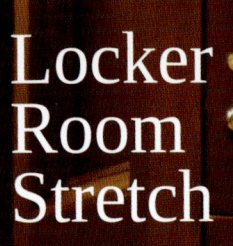

Extend your leg on a low bench. If this feels awesome, windshield your leg side-to-side, and then flex/extend the ankle. You may also feel this stretch in the inner hip and calf muscles.

Hamstrings & Ankles

> ## *How often should I stretch?*

Everyday. It does not mean stretch every muscle in the body. Instead, focus on one area, such as your ankles and calves. The next day, focus on the neck. Stretching on the course after a few holes is one of my favorite ways to get the daily stretch in. While on the course, I do not hold for more than 15-20 seconds.

Lats, Shoulders & Upper Back

Support great golf posture, as well as backswing arm elevation.

Stand close to a wall with your arms flush against it. Maintain a quiet back as you extend the arms up overhead, and then back down.

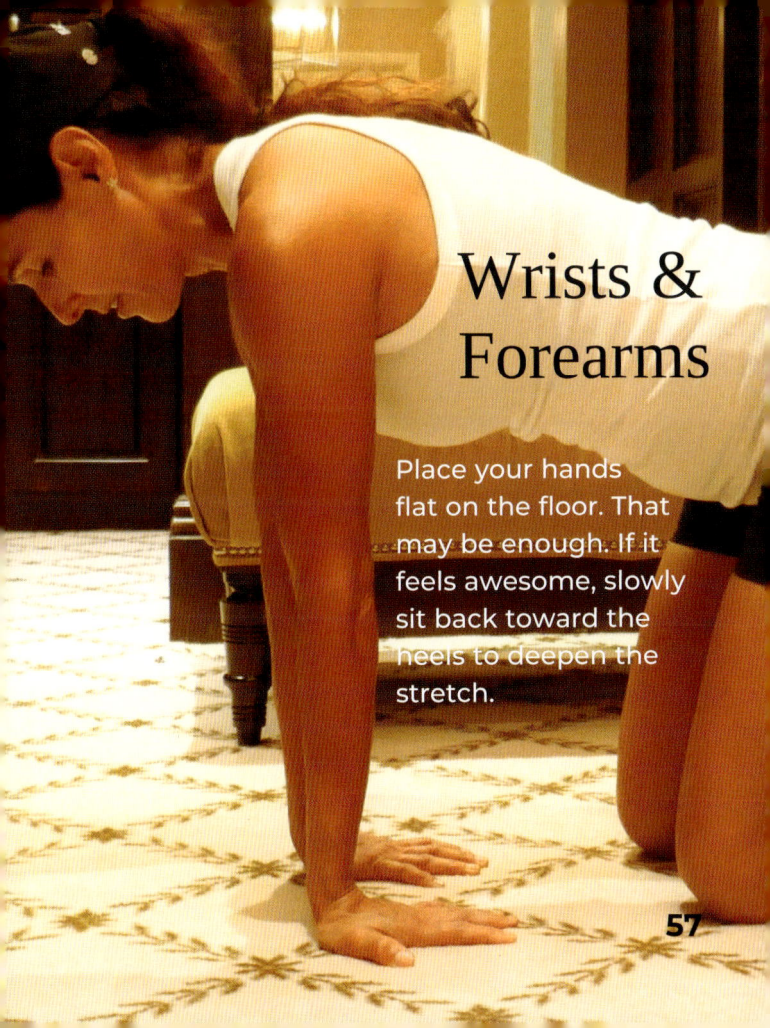

Wrists & Forearms

Place your hands flat on the floor. That may be enough. If it feels awesome, slowly sit back toward the heels to deepen the stretch.

Cat-Cow for Spine

Improve flexibility of the neck, shoulders and spine.

Chest & Arm Opener

Focus your breath into the target muscle.

Place one hand on the wall. Rotate in the opposite direction of the wall to feel a stretch in the entire pectoral region, as well as the interior of the arm. Perform slowly. You may find that just placing the hand on the wall is enough. Again, never force a stretch.

Targets the psoas, quad and ankle.

Foam rolling is a self-myofascial release (SMR) technique. It helps release stuck fascia and adhesions from the muscle that limit range of motion. Roll daily for best results.

Psoas, Quad, Back & Legs

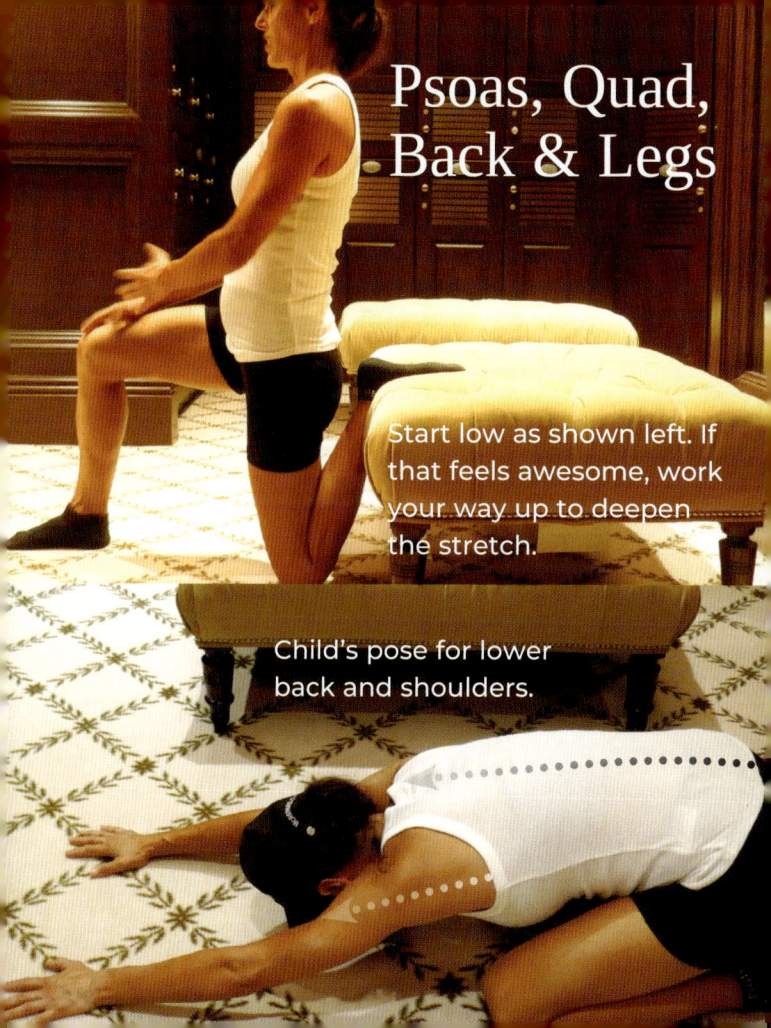

Start low as shown left. If that feels awesome, work your way up to deepen the stretch.

Child's pose for lower back and shoulders.

At the Gym

> *Should I do anything specific at the gym for golf?*

Golf is a demanding sport. To optimize performance and stay injury-free, focus on these areas:

MOBILITY:
Focus on one body part each day to improve and maintain range of motion. Target rotational stretches.

LOWER BODY STRENGTH:
Focus on compound exercises that target multiple muscle groups, such as squats, deadlifts, and step-ups. Also, focus on rotational moves and single leg exercises.

UPPER BODY STRENGTH:
Focus on the back muscles, wrists, forearms and grip strength. Exercises include push-ups, pull-ups, dumbbell rows, bicep and forearm curls, and grip holds.

SPEED:
Focus on training bursts of speed such as jump squats and sprinting.

KEEP YOUR BRAIN HAPPY

Nutrition Tips

- Eat a big breakfast to fuel the day.

- Bring nutritional snacks, such as power bars or nut bars. Or make your own!

- Snack often during the round to keep energy levels up.

- Hydrate often to keep your muscles and brain happy. Dehydration greatly affects decision making and performance.

- Avoid high sugar snacks, as these can affect your performance.

WHAT TO LOOK FOR IN
Protein Bars

A protein bar should have no more than 14 grams of sugar per serving and about five grams of fiber, which helps you digest it slowly and release its energy evenly. A bar labeled as a Protein Bar should have at least 8-10 grams of protein.

ON THE COURSE
Hydration

I admit that I am a water snob. I prefer water that is clean-tasting and non-mineral. The exception is San Pellegrino water. **What is your favorite water?** Some folks do not like to drink water. If that is the case, there are many healthy choices to keep you hydrated without all the sugar, and preferably in a glass bottle. Incorporate raw Kombucha in the mix for a healthy gut. It is fermented and bubbly passed down through centuries of Eastern tradition. I love it!

> *Are the drinks that courses sell okay?*

Most drinks that you find in the cooler of golf courses are loaded with sugar. Excess sugar will spike your glucose levels, sending you very high, then very low. This is not a good recipe for your golf round.

Total Fat 0g		0%
Sodium 270mg		12%
Total Carbohydrate 36g		13%
Total Sugars 34g	*Uh-oh!*	
Includes 34g Added Sugars		69%
Protein 0g		
Potassium 80mg		0%

Not a significant source of saturated fat, trans fat, cholesterol, dietary fiber, vitamin D, calcium, and iron.

Water, sugar, dextrose, citric acid, salt, sodium citrate, monopotassium phosphate, gum arabic, natural flavor, sucrose acetate isobutyrate, glycerol ester of rosin, yellow 6.

> *How much time should I allocate for practice?*

The answer to this question will guide the amount of practice required to improve your game, as well as the number of lessons with a golf professional. I recommend as much as possible. Just 10 minutes in the backyard with foam balls can be beneficial. Quality practice and practice often. The amount of practice will also depend on your goals. For example, if your goal is to be a single-digit handicap player, and you have ample time to practice and can play weekly, then that may be an achievable goal. If on the other hand, you'd like to be a single-digit player but work full time, have three kids and do not take lessons or like to practice, achieving that goal may not happen. Most players are smart. They get what is required to be a single-digit. Most players do not care to go that low. They are happy striking the ball well, having fun with their pals with a goal of breaking 100 or 90.

Practice Time

Practice in the backyard with foam balls.

TOP 5
Performance Tips

TIP #1
CONSISTENT ROUTINES

A consistent pre-shot and post-shot routine is your pal. It keeps you focused and your nerves at bay by occupying the mind. A routine by nature is performing the same thought-pattern process to optimize performance.

One Strong Feel

" *Swing out to 2.*
I got this!

TIP #2
CREATE MANTRAS

Confidence begins with a confident swing. Players who are struggling with their swing cannot *really* play the game, because their focus is on the swing. I recommend only one or two strong swing feels. Any more than one or two can interrupt performance. Create a mantra for your feel.

A poor shot is an opportunity.

YES

**TIP #3
OPPORTUNITY**
Even if the ball dribbles down the fairway, finish like it was the best shot ever, and then learn from it. The brain learns from mistakes, otherwise there is no reference point.

NO

The Post-Shot Routine is as important as the Pre-Shot Routine. Your feelings and self-talk after a shot play a significant role in your performance on that day, and in future rounds.

Take a breath between shots.

When and How to Focus

TIP #4
FOCUS

When I was learning the game, I thought that I had to be focused for the entire round. Thank goodness that is not required. Focus takes a lot of energy! When your turn is up, focus. When you've hit the shot, turn it off. Between shots, enjoy your pals or have a snack while admiring the beautiful blue sky and the smell of fresh cut grass...and that par you just posted on the scorecard.

GOLF IS A BIG GARDEN
Enjoy Nature's Beauty

**TIP #5
ENJOY NATURE**
Take it all in when you're playing a round. Golf is a sport that offers limitless natural beauty.

77

Notes

SWING ESSENTIALS *START HERE*

79

80

An Awesome Grip

A proper grip allows the club to hinge and unhinge with ease. An awesome grip also helps to square the face at impact. Many players struggle with maintaining a proper grip. In this section, let's cover the essentials for a solid grip.

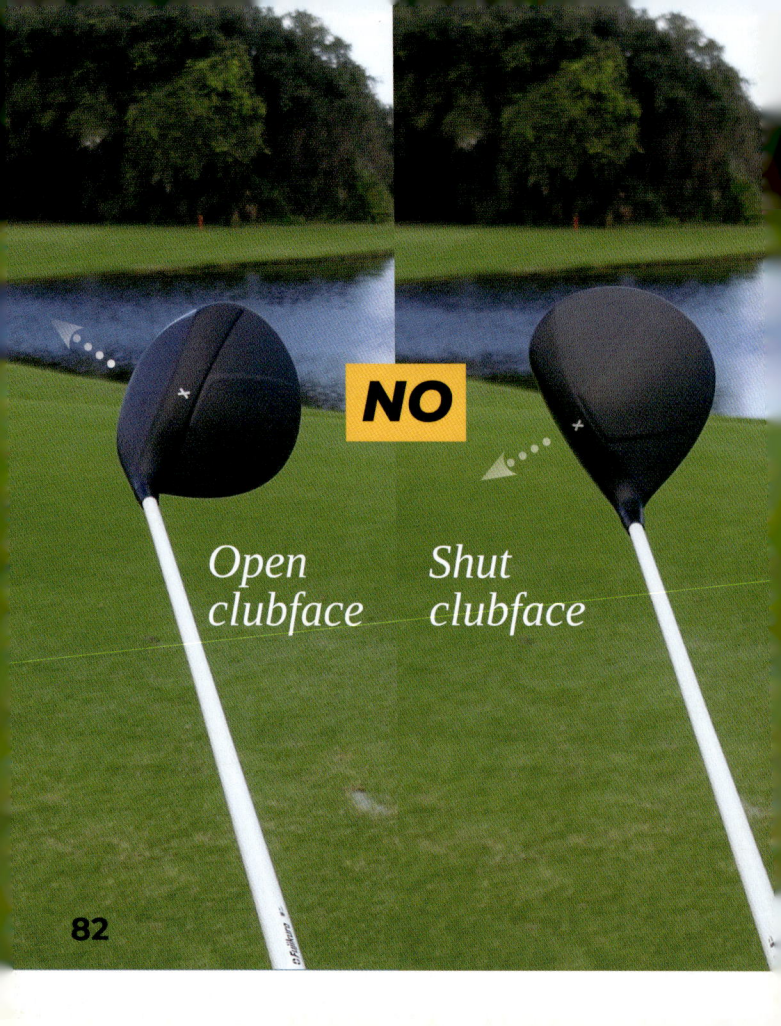

NO

Open clubface

Shut clubface

As you take your grip, pay attention to the clubface to make sure that it is square.

YES

Square clubface

STEP 1

Let's begin with the glove hand.

NO

Shaft is in the palm.

grip down about an inch

YES

Grip the club in the fingers with the index finger separated.

85

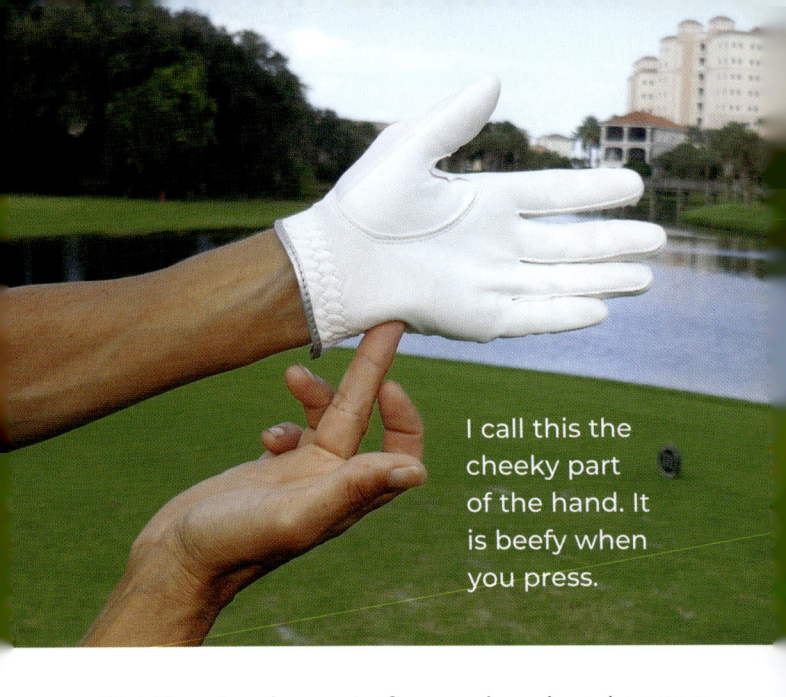

> I call this the cheeky part of the hand. It is beefy when you press.

Get the cheeky part of your glove hand on top of the shaft. I see players missing this aspect of the grip, quite often. The club is moving at 70-, 80-, upwards of 90-miles-per-hour, so it's important to have a well-supported grip.

YES

STEP 2

The cheeky part helps support the weight of the club.

NO

Too much in the palm.

With a neutral grip, the logo area of the glove is facing the target at impact.

Let's add the other hand

Your lead hand and clubface are pals. A neutral grip mirrors the clubface at impact where the logo on the glove is facing the target. A strong grip pre-sets the face square to slightly closed. A weak grip pre-sets the face open. I recommend a neutral to slightly stronger grip for most players.

This area hides the thumb of your glove hand.

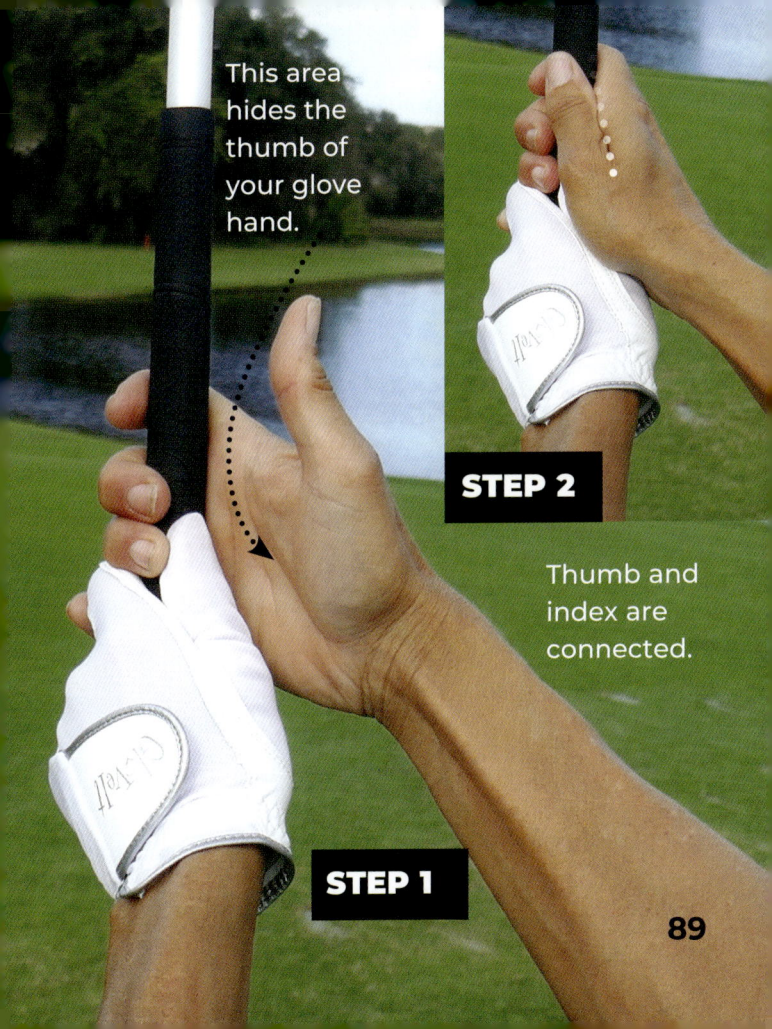

STEP 2

STEP 1

Thumb and index are connected.

STEP 3

Let's Connect Your Hands

Overlap Hands
Pinkie overlaps with the glove index finger.

Stacked Hands
Popular with small-handed players. This grip makes the club easier to hinge.

Interlocked Hands

Pinkie interlocks with the glove index finger. This is the grip that I use.

Experiment with all three to see what works best for you.

Neutral Grip

The Finished Grip

The line created by your thumb and index finger points the way. For most players, I recommend a neutral grip (to slightly strong). A weak grip will tend to keep the clubface open. A stronger grip will tend to create a more closed clubface.

Weak Grip

Strong Grip

STEP 1

Hold the club vertically. The club should feel light, including your grip pressure.

STEP 2

Hold the club parallel to the ground. The club should feel heavier and your grip pressure more firm.

STEP 3

Now with the contrast of too light and too heavy, hold the club at roughly 45 degrees. The grip should feel firm enough to support the weight of the club.

How to Determine Grip Pressure

One of the main reasons we wear a glove is to keep a firm hold on the club during the swing. If we are too firm, the club cannot hinge and unhinge. Plus, the club is moving upwards of 100 miles per hour, so it is important to have the right grip pressure.

UNDERSTANDING
Posture

There are two kinds of golf posture: Static and Dynamic.

In this section, let's identify the keys for both. ***Static*** posture is your address position. ***Dynamic*** posture is your swing's posture in motion. Posture is comprised of bends and tilts (rotation), which keeps the concept of posture simple.

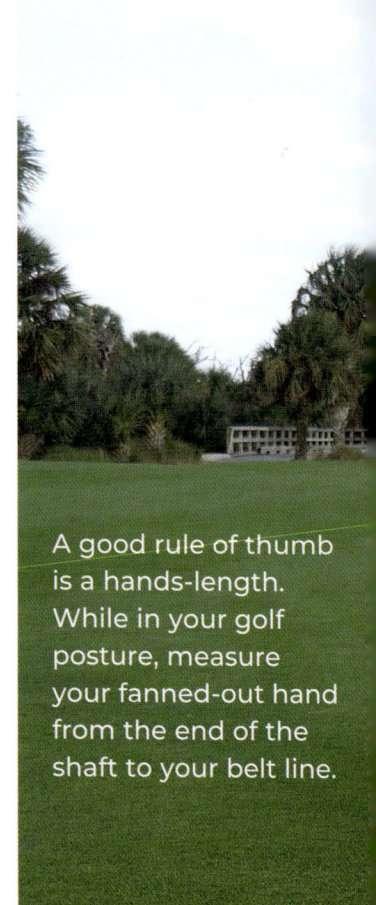

A good rule of thumb is a hands-length. While in your golf posture, measure your fanned-out hand from the end of the shaft to your belt line.

> *How far should I stand from the ball?*

Maintaining inclined angles throughout the swing is key for swing success.

GOLF POSTURE IS MADE UP OF
Bends & Tilts

A **_bend_** is defined as forward bend established by a hinge from the hip line. A **_tilt_** is defined as adding rotation and side bend to that forward bend to maintain the inclination of golf posture throughout the swing.

If the ball was chest high at address, we would not need the bends. But because the ball is on the ground, we need to bend forward to reach it. To strike it, we need to maintain these inclined angles throughout the swing. To feel and train great golf posture, let's hop on a flight.

What's Your Favorite Airline?

Mine is jetBlue as indicated by my blue outfit.

Posture on a Plane

To get a feel of golf posture, let's jump on your favorite airline and take flight. Simulating an airplane helps players feel the bends and tilts of the golf swing. Plus, it's a great pre-round warm-up.

STEP 1

Place your hands on the hip joints to hinge yourself into position.

Good torso tilts help to leverage the ground with a better hip rotation.

STEP 2
Spread your wings!

Flying your airplane creates the correct tilts during the backswing and downswing with the hips and the torso!

STEP 3
Take a sharp turn into the backswing.

STEP 4

Uh-oh! You forgot something at the gate, gotta whiz back.

This is actually side bend that creates the downward angle.

Spreading your wings helps to feel the downward shoulder line angle that we need during the backswing and downswing.

Level wings will create a backswing that is too flat.

NO

Missing side bend.

Shoulders too level.

NO

Many players are missing side bend in their backswing, resulting in what is referred to as *flat shoulder*

Use a club to guide a downward shoulder angle.

YES

The jetBlue progression with a club.

Stand tall and slide the trail arm down your leg. This creates downswing side bend.

Downswing forward and side bend

As you rotate through, maintain a downward shoulder angle.

Posture Setup Keys

- Neutral spine
- Hinge from hips
- Armpits in line with knees
- Arms slightly extended away from body
- Slight knee flex

As a result of your grip, there is a slight side bend at setup, where your trail arm is lower.

With driver, this is slightly increased with the sternum behind the clubhead.

NO

Both of these forward bends are incorrect. The edge of my shoulder is not in line with the knee caps.

NO

Not enough forward bend.

Too much forward bend.

YES

" *How much forward bend?*

An easy way to ensure enough forward bend is to align the edge of your shoulder with the knee caps.

117

NO

" What is a neutral spine?

Shuts off glutes and core.

Ouch!

Pelvis is tucked with a rounded back.

Pelvis is tilted downward, creating an excessive curve in the lower back.

Pelvis is neutral as is the spine. A neutral spine is simply your spine's natural curve. It is the safest position for your golf swing and lower back.

YES

Always swing in neutral.

Alignment

An easy way to visualize alignment is with the help of railroad tracks.

TARGET LINE

The ball is on one track (your target line) and your body is aligned on the other track (parallel and left).

BODY LINES

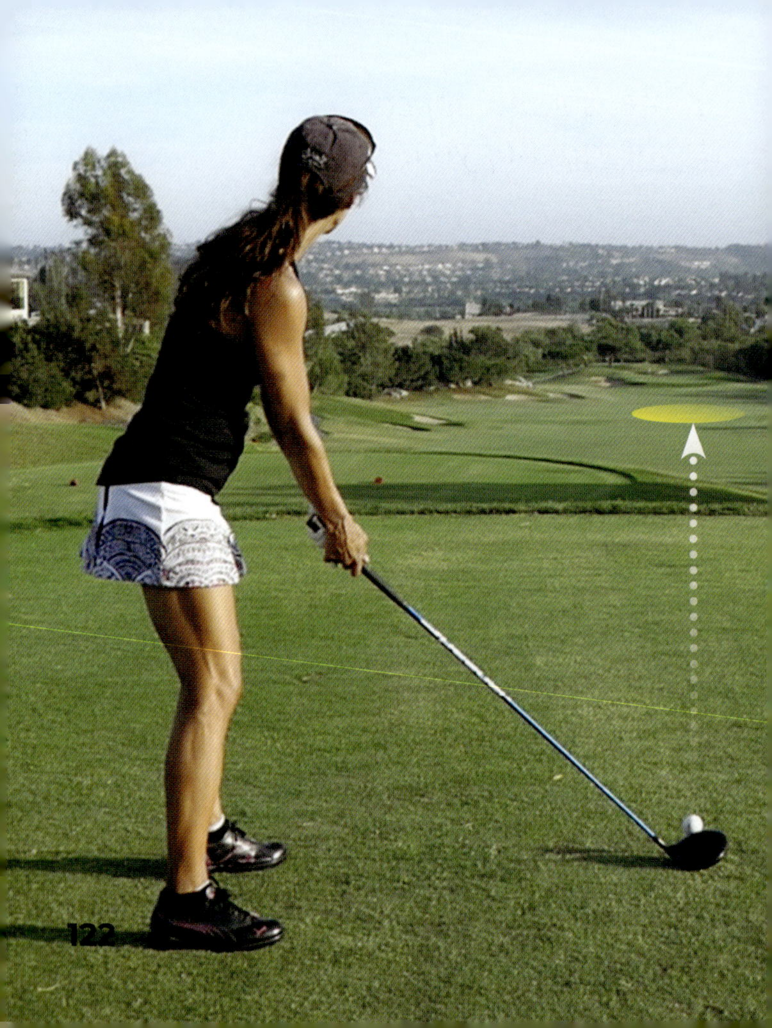

Target should appear to the right of you.

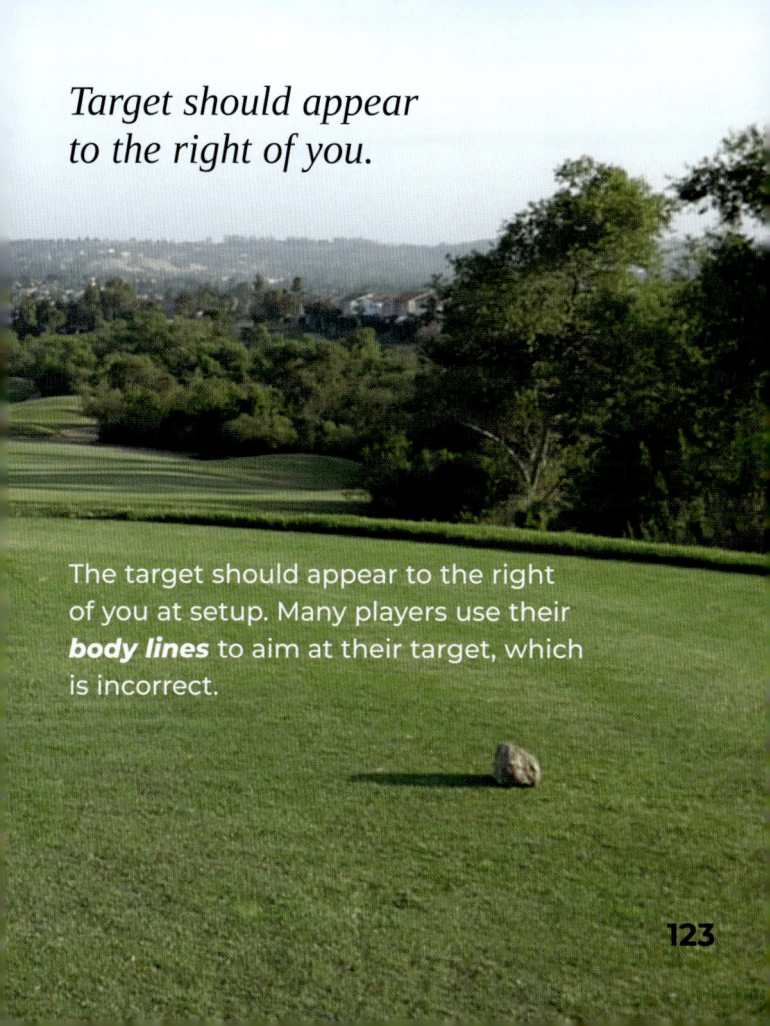

The target should appear to the right of you at setup. Many players use their ***body lines*** to aim at their target, which is incorrect.

OPEN SETUP

Body lines are left of a parallel setup.

An open setup is handy for creating fade ball flights. Around the green, it creates a higher lofted shot that stops on a dime.

SQUARE SETUP

Body lines are parallel to the target line.

A square setup is how you'll address most of your shots.

Notes

SETUP

ESSENTIALS

Club Setups

In this section, we'll cover setup with the driver all the way down to the wedge.

Setup sets the stage for a successful, effortless swing. As a newer player, your goal is to groove setups from driver to wedge. The setups change due to the length of the shaft. Length changes the club's low point (where it bottoms out), which is why we adjust setup.

> *" Why do we tee it up for the driver?*

The driver is the longest club in the bag. The ball is teed up because we swing upward through the ball. The ball complements this upward attack angle by being placed off the heel of the front foot.

This wedge represents the driver's upward angle through the ball.

129

NO

Spine angled toward target.

Be mindful of your head position at setup. I see this a lot, where the head is leaning toward the target.

This promotes a Reverse Spine backswing, which promotes back pain and a steep downswing, producing a slice, weak-right, pull or topped shot.

Head Position

YES

Place the head in line with your spine to promote a pain-free backswing.

Sternum Position
WITH DRIVER

Too High

NO

Ball is too far back with the sternum over, or ahead of the ball, which opens the shoulders and creates a shoulder line that is too level.

YES

Ball positioned off of lead heel. Sternum (spine) positioned behind the clubhead. This squares you up and creates a launch shoulder angle.

133

WEDGE TO 7-IRON

Sternum is over the ball.

HYBRIDS

For hybrids replacing the longer irons (6- to 4-iron, sternum is over the clubhead. Hybrids replacing 7-iron, sternum is over the ball.

NO

Too close

Too far away

Distance from the ball affects balance points. Too close will place your balance points toward the toes. Too far, in your heels.

YES

Distance from the Ball APPLIES FOR ALL CLUBS

Using your hand and while in golf posture, measure a full hands-length from the end of the shaft to your belt line.

Stance Width

NO

Too wide restricts body movement through the swing.

138

YES

Just outside of hip-width with your fairway clubs. Driver will be outside of shoulder-width.

Balance Points in Feet

NO

Avoid the extremes: too much in the toe or heel.

140

YES

Balance points over laces of shoe is a good rule of thumb for all your clubs.

141

NO

Handle is too far forward (a forward press). A press affects the downswing's attack angle and clubface's loft.

Handle
Position
WITH DRIVER

YES

Handle in line with the hands to maintain the club's loft.

143

NO

Hands too far forward, which delofts the face, creating low ball flights.

Ball is too far back, creating lower ball flights.

144

IRONS & HYBRIDS

YES

Handle of the shaft is in line to slightly ahead of the ball at setup.

NO

Hands too far forward, which delofts the face creating low ball flights.

Ball is too far back. This can create lower ball flights.

YES

WOOD

Sternum positioned in line with the edge of the clubhead. Ball positioned off the lead chest. Hands are in line with shaft to maintain the club's loft.

147

Ball Position

Ball position with all these clubs is in the center of the stance. The exception would be for a low running chip or low trajectory pitch, where you'd play the back of center.

WEDGE TO
7-IRON

6-IRON & HYBRIDS

Ball position with all these clubs is ahead of center. The exception would be for a hybrid replacing your 7- through 9-iron. Ball position would then be center.

Hybrids vs. Woods

HYBRIDS

Hybrids are not Woods

Ball with hybrids (replacing the 6- to 3-iron) is positioned just ahead of center.

WOODS

Woods are second in command to the driver in shaft length. Ball is positioned off the lead chest where a golf shirt logo would be.

Ball Positions

Ball back for a lower trajectory.

Ball ahead to create a higher ball flight.

Wedge Setup for Chips

- Sternum slightly ahead of ball to create a consistent low point.

- Hands slightly ahead

- Narrow stance

- More weight on lead leg

More about this in the chip section.

Notes

LET'S SWING STEP-BY-STEP SWING PROGRESSIONS

157

WHAT IS
Swing Plane?

Before we begin our swing progression skills, let's first understand the swing's radius. ***The club swings on an invisible tilted circle.*** The goal is to keep the clubhead on that imaginary tilted circle throughout the swing. We do this with a proper setup for the club in hand, as well as maintaining a connected swing back and through.

158

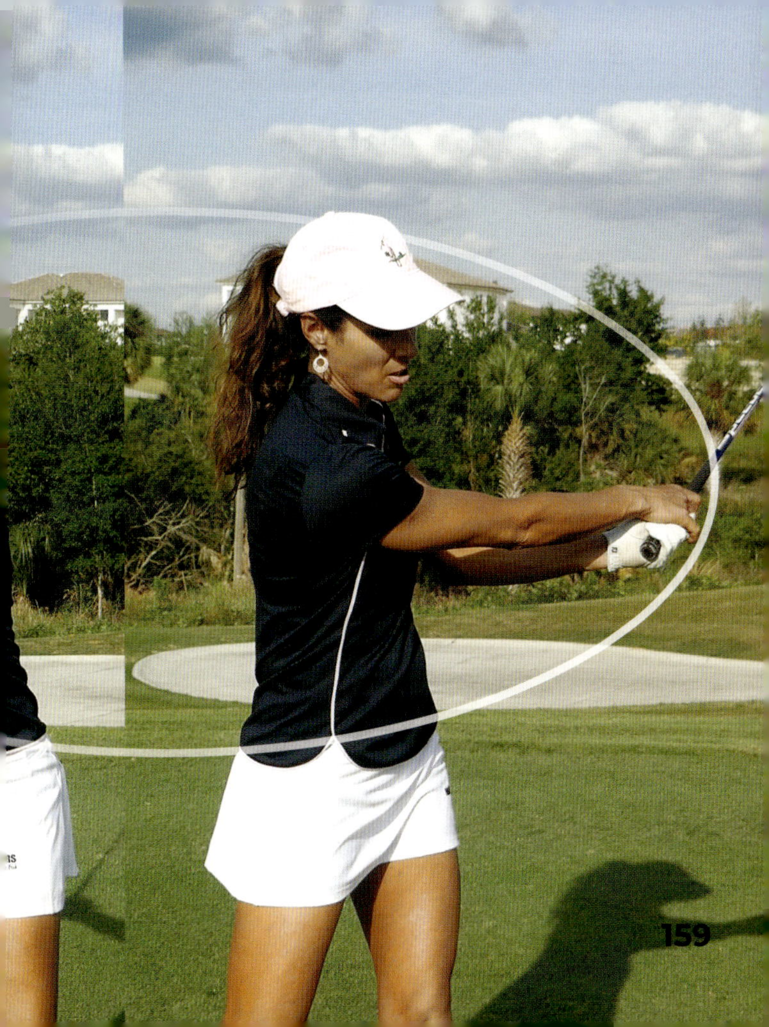

Use a shaft to guide the way.

NO

Players fall off the swing plane with a steep downswing. The club's shaft becomes too vertical during the downswing.

A fun way to practice the swing plane!

YES

The club's angle during the backswing and downswing should point toward the target line.

161

Takeaway Keys

The takeaway is just that. We are taking the club away from the address position.

Let's kick-off the swing (assuming a proper setup and clear understanding of the swing plane) with a connected takeaway. The takeaway is a big deal. It sets the club on or off plane right out of the gate. A great takeaway makes the backswing and downswing much easier.

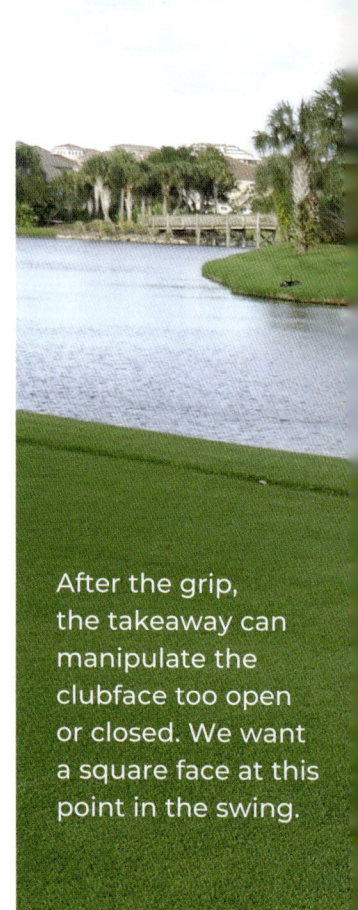

After the grip, the takeaway can manipulate the clubface too open or closed. We want a square face at this point in the swing.

The clubace mirrors the spine angle indicating a square face.

NO

Clubface is opening.

Forearms are over-rolling, sending the club too inside and opening the clubface.

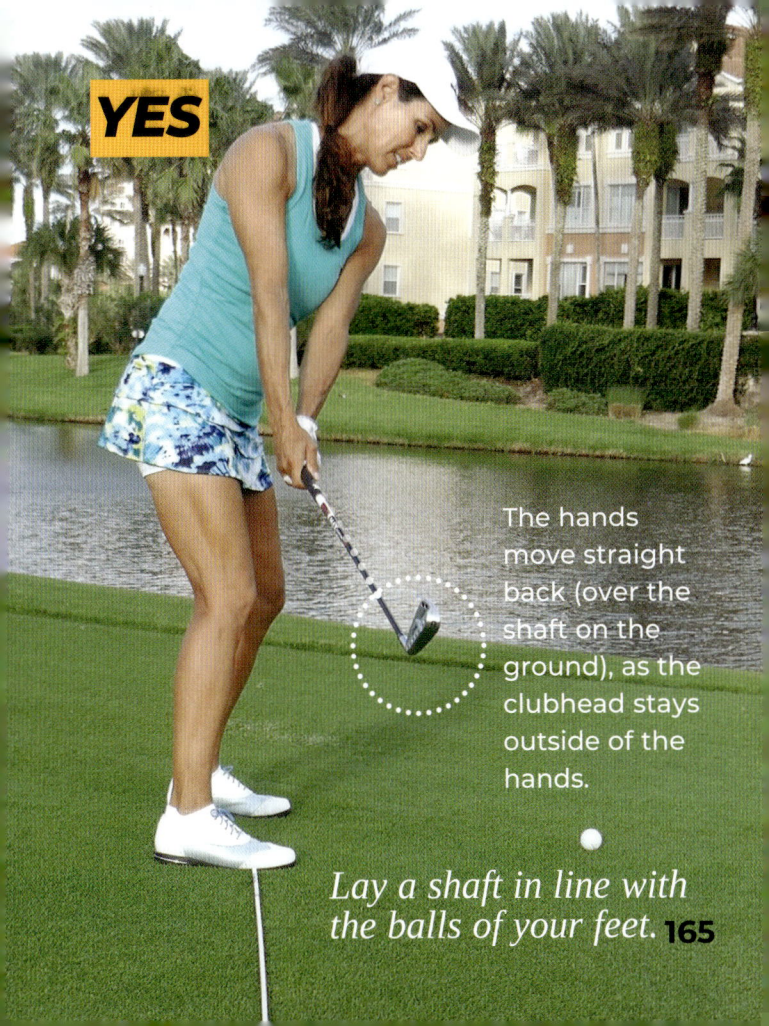

YES

The hands move straight back (over the shaft on the ground), as the clubhead stays outside of the hands.

Lay a shaft in line with the balls of your feet. **165**

166

Visualize a triangle to groove a connected takeaway.

A great visual to learn a connected takeaway.

167

Takeaway Culprits

A Big Gap

NO

As the hands move away from the body, the lead arm is disconnected from the torso. This affects balance points toward the toes. As a result, the backswing will most likely be off plane.

YES

Stay Connected

As the hands stay close to the body, the lead arm stays connected to the torso. From here, the club hinges vertically.

NO

facing down

The ballmarker on my glove is facing the ground, which shuts the face, creating too much flexion in the lead wrist.

YES

facing outward

Focus on the glove's logo/ballmarker as your guide. It should face outward, not down.

Backswing Culprits

NO

Over-flexed wrist with bent arms.

Newer players over-flex the lead wrist. It often begins right out of the gate, during the takeaway.

YES

Instead, we want a straight arm with a fairly flat wrist for a square face (assuming a neutral to slightly strong grip).

NO

This swing is missing structure and is a popular culprit among newer players. Players over-rotate the hips with collapsed arms.

YES

Instead, grip the ground with your spiked golf shoes to create a stable base to rotate your torso around. Maintain long arms for a wide swing arc.

Golf shoes have spikes to help create friction with the ground.

175

Structure Begins Here

Zip the upper arms to the torso.

Your body is the swing's engine.

STEP 1
The first step to creating structure is connection. Connecting the upper arms to the torso provides a solid foundation.

Learn how to swing with the body rather than the arms. Most newer players use only the arms.

177

START WITH SMALL SWINGS

STEP 2
Now that we have structure, let's swing. Learning to first use the body correctly is most important.

Hands no higher than waist height.

Rotate through.

Plus, you'll groove these 35- to 45-yard pitch shots around the green at the same time!

STEP 3

As the swings get a little bigger, the goal still is to promote a body pivot back and through.

Maintain your arm-to-chest connection throughout the swing to encourage a body pivot (versus using just the arms).

At the Range

12

9

8

Clock Swings

Visualize a clock. Hands no higher than 9, but FEEL 8 in the real swing. Otherwise, you may end up at noon with the hands .

Lead side firm for solid strikes.

Long arms on the through-swing, finishing tall and balanced.

183

NO

Turn the Torso

Torso hasn't rotated.

184

YES

Torso has rotated and the spine is angled away from the target.

185

NO

Lead side is collapsed.

YES

A Strong Finish

Lead side is firm and strong, which allows the club to maximize its speed.

Focus on the back shoulder.

A great feel is to focus on the trail shoulder striking the ball.

This cue helps players swing through (versus hitting and stopping).

Create an L shape during the backswing...

STEP 1

During the backswing, the lead arm is long with the club hinged. The club and lead arm form a crisp L shape.

Single Arm Practice

Isolate each arm to groove a solid swing.

and through-swing.

STEP 2
Now with the trail arm, swing through. The torso has rotated. The trail arm is long and the club has re-hinged on the through-swing, creating a crisp L shape.

STEP 3

Now with both hands on the club, visualize long arms, creating that crisp L shape during the backswing...

...and the through-swing.

> *What is the release?*

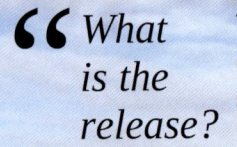

The release is the unhinging of the wrists as they rotate to square then close the clubface.

Release Practice

STEP 1
From thigh to thigh the club should release. To practice this, begin at waist height.

Lead hand knuckles roll down.

194

Newer (and even experienced) players struggle with rotating (supinating) the lead arm during the follow-through.

STEP 2
Swing through, then let go with the trail arm to isolate the lead arm, rotating away from the ball.

Releasing the club, where it is square at impact, and then closes.

Glove hand is on top pre-impact.

STEP 3
With both hands on the club, focus on the release.

From thigh to thigh, the club should release.

Trail hand is now on top of the glove hand.

Release the clubhead by rotating the forearms/wrists through the strike zone.

Rotation vs. Sway

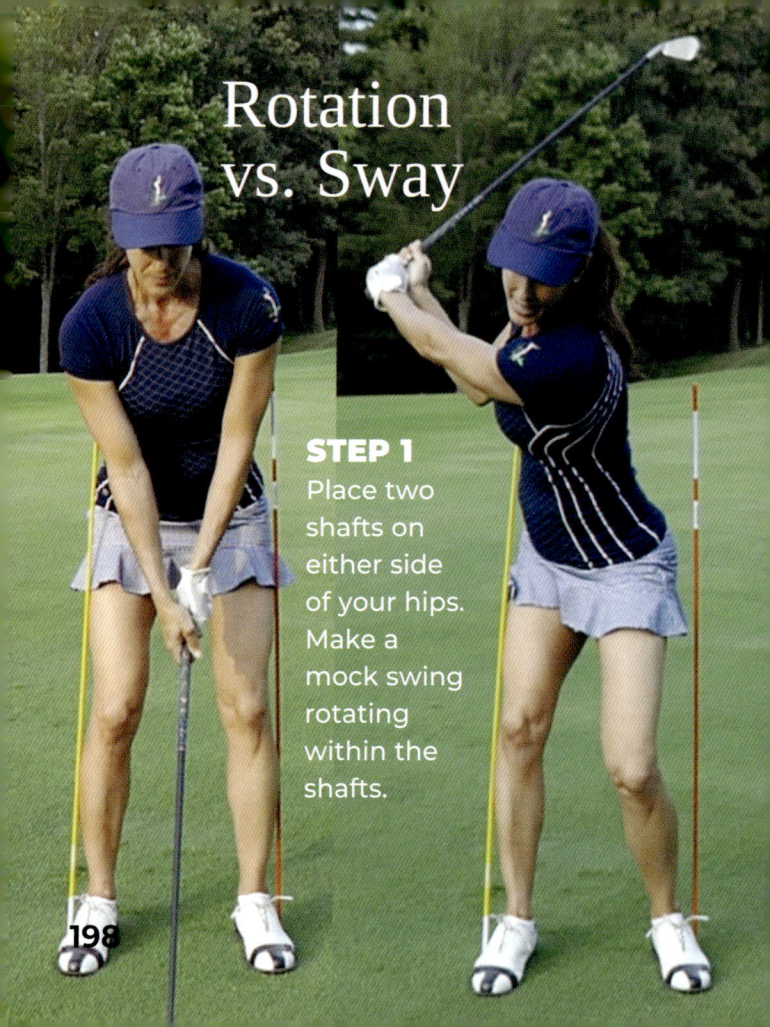

STEP 1
Place two shafts on either side of your hips. Make a mock swing rotating within the shafts.

STEP 2
Swing through with long arms rotating within the front shaft.

Lead side firm for solid strikes.

NO

Moving too lateral into the backswing.

YES

Instead, rotate within the shaft.

201

NO

Moving too lateral during the downswing.

202

YES

Instead, rotate within the shaft on the downswing.

203

On the Course

Around the Green

Bring that same connected swing to the course, always rotating all the way through.

From the Fairway

It's the same connected swing with your irons and hybrids.

Glove hand is hidden.

Forearms rotating to release the club.

Wood Swing. It is all the same connected swing.

Rotate all the way through.

Off the Tee

210

The same swing with the driver.

This keeps the swing repeatable and consistent!

Notes

LET'S TEE OFF LAUNCH THIS PUPPY

213

TEE OFF ESSENTIALS

Target & Routine

Nerves are a natural part of the game.

The key to success is to occupy the mind with positive and focused attention. Attention on where you would like the ball to land out in the fairway. Craft a consistent routine that you'll use for every shot. The more consistent, the better chances for shot success.

> *I get so nervous on the first tee. Any tips?*

As you prepare to hit your tee shot, it is important to focus on a target out in the fairway. The act of engaging the mind on the target leaves no space for fear or nerves.

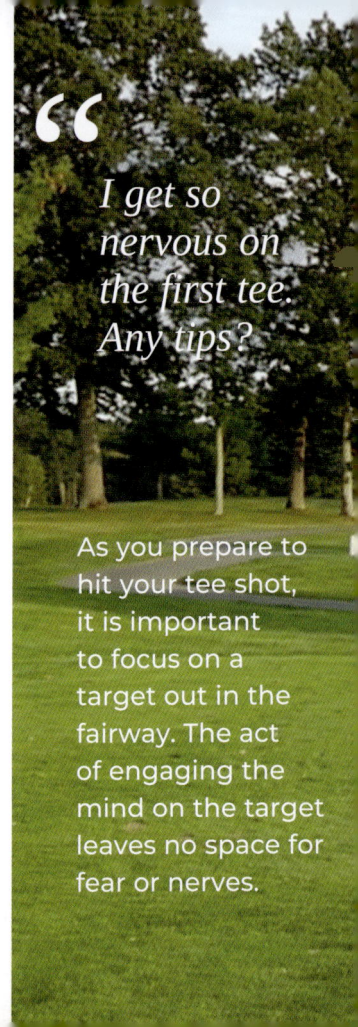

215

Confident Routine

As you take fluid practice swings from behind the ball looking out toward the target, visualize the ball landing in your intended area.

Calm the nerves with focus and an "I got this!" attitude.

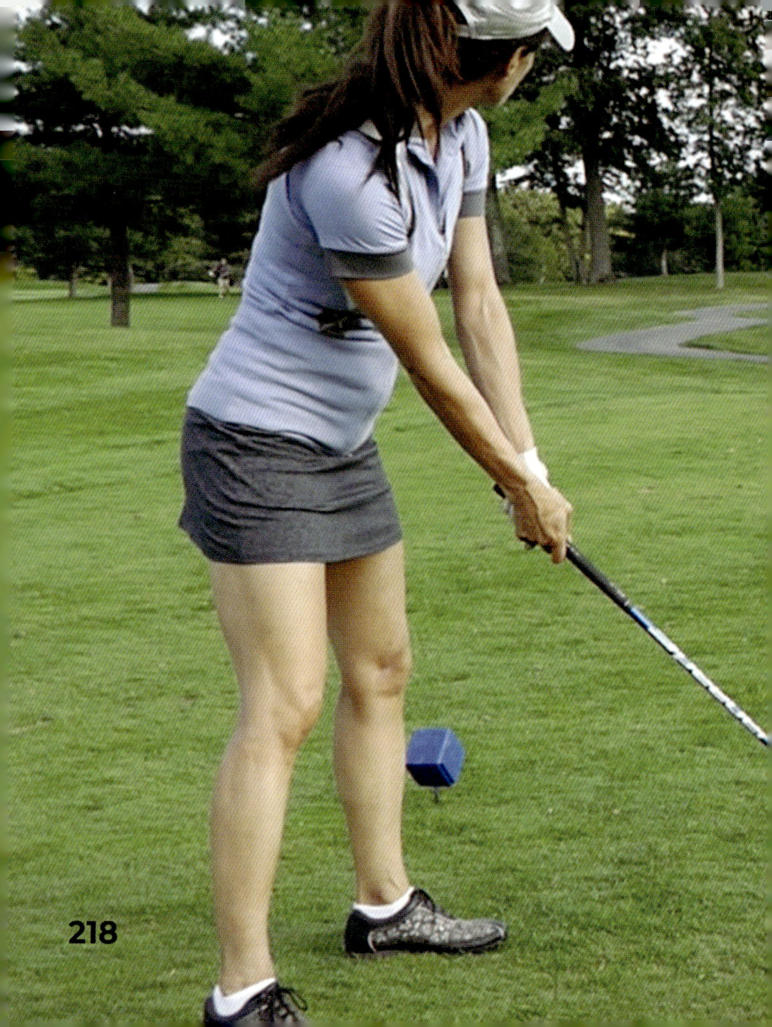

landing area

Alignment Process

To ensure spot-on alignment, select an intermediate target (a spot very close to your clubface), rather than trying to aim at spot way out in the distance.

Aim at a spot close to the clubface.

The Neck Crane

Uh-Oh! Where ya going?

I see this a ton in my camps. Players address the ball and proceed to crane their neck 360 degrees to look at their intended target. That is a clue that your alignment is a tad off. Oftentimes, too far right (for most players).

Instead, while in your posture, swivel your head to view the target. If your alignment is square, there should be no need to crane the neck.

Fear of Water

Successfully manage the fear of water.

Notice the water, yes. However, direct your energies beyond the water to your target area where you would like the ball to land. Occupying the mind with directed focus produces amazing results.

NO

Too High

Tee Heights

Too Low

NO

OTHER CLUBS

Tee it up just above the turf for irons and slightly higher for hybrids and woods.

DRIVER TEE HEIGHT

YES

A good rule of thumb is half the ball above the top half of the driver.

Driver Setup Keys

- Sternum in line with the back of the clubhead creating an angled shoulder line

- Width of stance is slightly outside shoulder-width

- Ball positioned off of lead heel

- Neutral spine
- Armpit area in line with knees
- Arms slightly extended away from body
- Slight knee flex
- Feet pressure points over laces of shoe

Driver Swing Keys

Creating width with long arms during the takeaway. Clubhead is furthest away from body at this point. Front shoulder moving down and toward the trail side with leg pressure moving into trail leg.

75%

45°

Maintaining long arms while rotating hips roughly 45 degrees. This rotation helps to leverage the ground, making it easy to move into the downswing.

During the downswing, my hips rotate away from the ball (just like we practiced with the shaft drill).

Head is quiet to allow the club to extend with long arms with the front leg braced.

Trail shoulder and hips continuing to rotate away from the target line.

232

Tall and balanced with the trail foot on the toes.

Notes

FAIRWAY ESSENTIALS LET'S GET AIRBORNE

235

FROM THE FAIRWAY
Divots

Don't be afraid of divots.

Newer players don't like to take divots. They are fearful of fat shots, hurting their wrists or messing up the grass. But divots are a part of the game. The keys to successful divots are: correct ball position, an on-plane swing, transfer of pressure and a full finish.

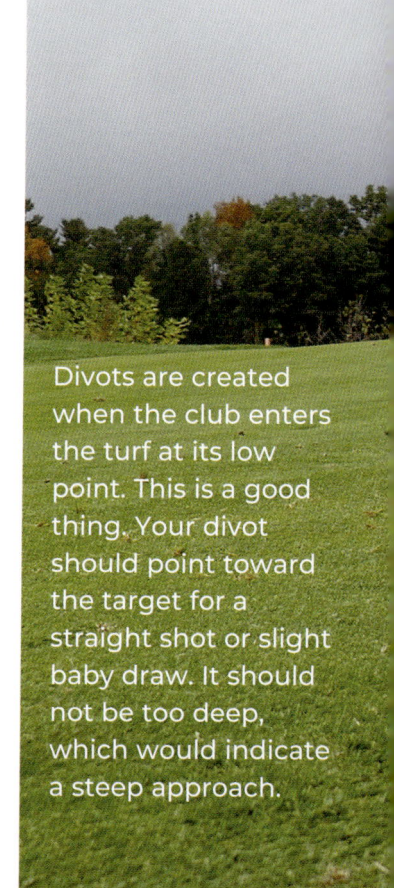

Divots are created when the club enters the turf at its low point. This is a good thing. Your divot should point toward the target for a straight shot or slight baby draw. It should not be too deep, which would indicate a steep approach.

THIS IS A GOOD DIVOT.

237

According to the USGA, properly repairing divots helps the turf recover as quickly as possible and also restores a smooth playing surface. An unrepaired divot can take months to heal, and it may never fully recover. Repairing divots maintains good course playability for your fellow golfers and sets a positive example for them as well.

How to Replace a Divot

If the divot is intact and soil is still attached to it, simply replace it in the correct orientation, and then firmly press the divot into the ground with your foot. This establishes good contact between the turf roots and soil, which helps the divot heal.

SOURCE: USGA.com

How to Fill a Divot

When using divot mix, it is important to avoid over- or under-filling divots. Over-filled divots will damage mowing equipment and create poor playing conditions. Under-filling a divot will result in a depression that can affect the lie of ball. The correct way is to add mix until it is slightly below the height of the adjacent turf, and then smooth it out and press down with your foot.

The Swing Arc

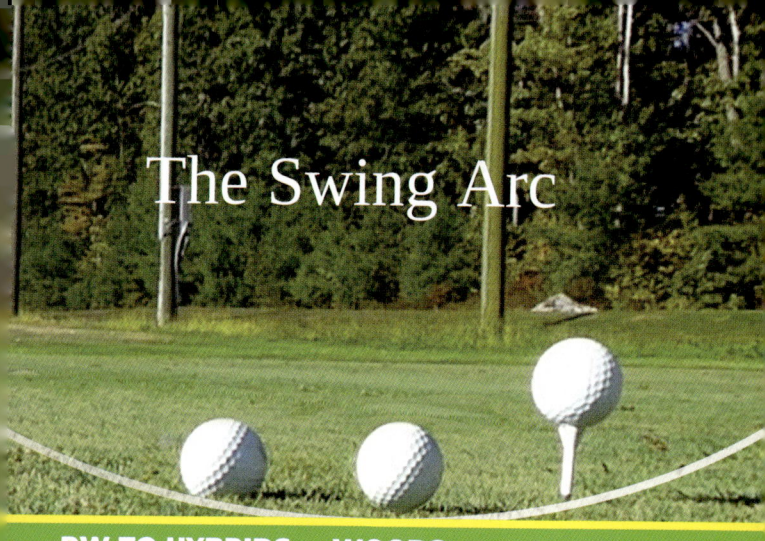

PW TO HYBRIDS
Approach is down.

WOODS
Approach is level.

DRIVER
Approach is up.

The golf swing is an arc. The lowest part of the swing is the bottom of the arc. The key to consistent ball striking is creating a consistent low point. This low point changes based on the club in hand. Woods swing at the lowest point which is why there is typically no divot.

Approach is more level with the wood

Players who never take any divot most likely strike the ball thin. For irons and hybrids, the approach is a downward strike. The driver requires an upward strike. A level approach is needed for woods. This is why ball position is paramount to complement the club in hand.

NO

Help Factor

This is a very popular culprit among newer players. They try to help the ball in the air, which results in a topped or fat shot.

YES

Players try to *get under the ball*. Instead, strike down and through.

NO

Too level

When on the course, watch the shoulder line. If it gets too level during the backswing or downswing, you may mis-hit the shot.

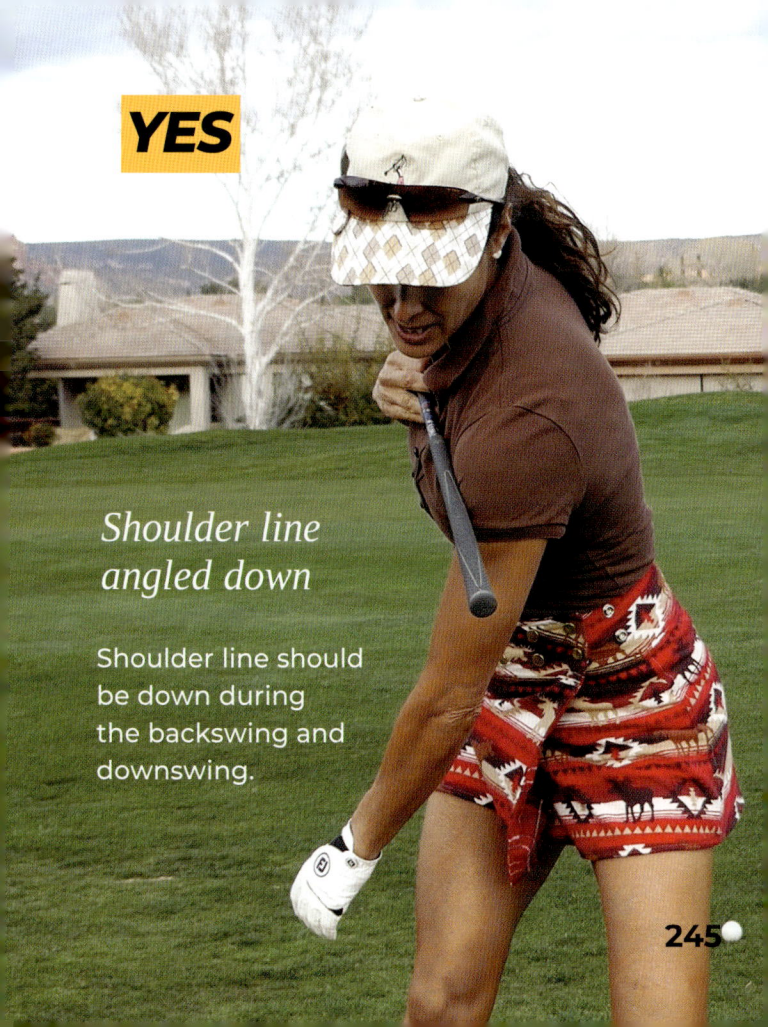

YES

Shoulder line angled down

Shoulder line should be down during the backswing and downswing.

Focus on your shoulder line for solid strikes from the fairway.

Shoulder line angled down

SIMPLIFY
Impact

Lead hand and clubface are pals!

With a neutral grip, the logo on your glove mirrors the clubface.

249

Face-to-Wrist Relationship

Square clubface

YES

A neutral grip has a natural slight cup.

250

251

NO

Shut clubface

Players who flatten the lead wrist at the top of the swing with a strong grip close the clubface.

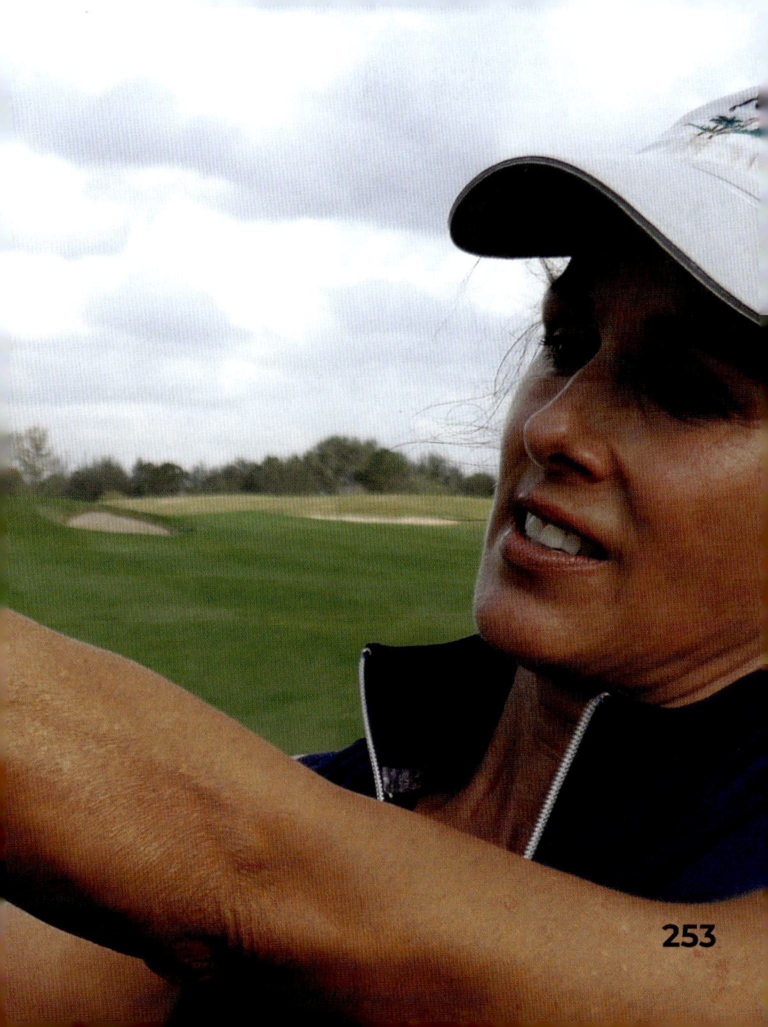

STEPS TO GREAT
Impact

It's all about impact, especially as it relates to the swing.

Everything—from your clubs, ball, setup and takeaway to your backswing and downswing—leads to the big moment when you strike the ball. Let's groove impact with the help of a kitchen spatula.

Grab a spatula from the kitchen and let's groove impact.

With a neutral grip, the lead hand and clubface match.

255

Impact Practice

Coming into the strike zone, the clubface is pointing slightly down.

256

The knuckles of the glove hand roll down to the ground to help square the clubface.

knuckles roll down

257

more forearm rotation

More forearm rotation is required to release the club with the face slightly open coming into the strike zone.

less forearm rotation

Ballmarker on glove is facing down, which requires less forearm rotation. It is easier and more consistent to square the face this way.

Roll the forearms and wrists downward to square and close the face.

Logo on glove is facing toward the target (neutral grip).

Trail hand is now on top.

261

The logo on the glove of your lead hand is facing the target and mirrors the clubface angle at impact.

Trail hand on top. I am allowing the full release of the club to create lots of speed and extension through the shot.

THE IMPORTANCE OF
Swing Plane

An on-plane swing makes it easy to deliver the club to the ball.

A swing that is off-plane, where the shaft is too far above or below the shaft plane line, will result in body compensations to square the face. Compensations are not an efficient way to build a repeatable swing. Work with a golf professional to groove your swing plane.

I am on-plane as I move into the downswing with my hands and club on the shaft plane line. The shaft of the club is angled toward the target line.

SHAFT PLANE LINE

Swing Keys

SOLID SETUP & TAKEAWAY

Ball position is ahead of center for this 19° hybrid. Hands are in line with the shaft, with a shoulder-width stance.

Connected takeaway with the arms, club and chest moving as one with solid legs and feet (gripping the ground).

TRANSFER PRESSURE

Moving pressure from backswing to downswing to generate lots of clubhead speed.

269

STAYING IN POSTURE

Releasing the club while staying in posture with the shoulder line angled down. Head is quiet, allowing the club to speed on by for great extension.

270

TALL FINISH

Full finish with back foot on its toe. Torso is tall and balanced over a straight front leg.

Stay in posture…

The key with successful shots from the tee or fairway is staying in posture.

...throughout the swing.

Remember the ball is on the ground, so it is paramount to maintain your posture angles to promote a solid strike.

STAYING IN POSTURE

Releasing the club while staying in posture, with the shoulder line angled down. My pressure is moving to the front leg, as indicated by the back foot rolling in toward the front side.

FULL FINISH

Full finish with hips fully rotated left of the target. The back foot on its toe, and torso tall and balanced over a straight front leg.

Practice Pressure

with the help of an alignment stick

276

With a shaft, practice moving pressure from the back leg to front leg without rotation.

Rotate through and stand tall.

TEE IN LINE WITH BALL

STEP 1
Lay a tee in line with the ball to identify your club's low point.

Practice Low Point
with the help of a tee

STEP 2

The divot should be just after the ball.

Woods

> *I top my woods...a lot!*

The woods are second in command to the driver, making them the most challenging clubs from the fairway.

The woods like to be swept up off the turf with little or no divot. Many players get too steep/vertical with their attack angle and end up hitting the ball thin or fat.

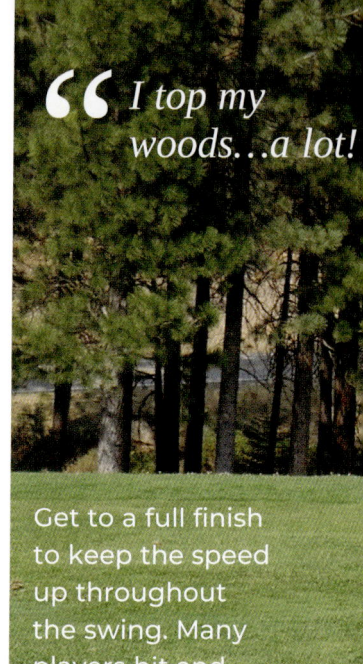

Get to a full finish to keep the speed up throughout the swing. Many players hit and stop, creating a chop style swing. The result is typically a chunked or topped shot.

281

Uh-Oh!

Arms are collapsing, which will create a vertical downswing.

NO

Get wide right from the start.

YES

283

NO

Uh-Oh!

Arms are bent. This shot will most likely be thin.

YES

Stay wide with your arms to create a long sweeping swing.

Notes

BUNKER GAME SPLASH WITH CONFIDENCE

287

WHAT IS
Bounce?

Bounce was designed by Gene Sarazen.

The bounce refers to the area of the golf club beneath the leading edge. It glides through the sand with ease.

Wedges typically have three types of bounce: low, mid, or high. As you progress in your game, I highly recommend getting fitted for your wedges.

Gene was an American professional golfer, one of the world's top players in the 1920s and 1930s, and the winner of seven major championships.

289

Square Clubface

A square clubface hides the bounce, allowing the leading edge to enter the sand. This is useful for firm or wet sand.

Open Clubface

An open clubface exposes the bounce and prevents the leading edge from digging.

An open setup is where the body lines are left of a square parallel setup. This creates a V shape.

Bunker Alignment

An open setup provides a slightly steeper angle of attack.

This promotes quick height out of the bunker. Players who swing too shallow with a square setup often blade it. Conversely, players who swing too steep often take too much sand.

Basic Bunker Shot

STEP 1
Open the clubface and stance line. Create a wide base with the handle low. A wider stance provides stability to create a consistent sand entry point. Position the ball ahead of center.

Before making a stroke, a player cannot touch the sand with the club.

Rules & Etiquette

STEP 2
Keeping the weight on your lead side, pivot the chest and hinge the club. Keep the hands low, but turn the torso.

295

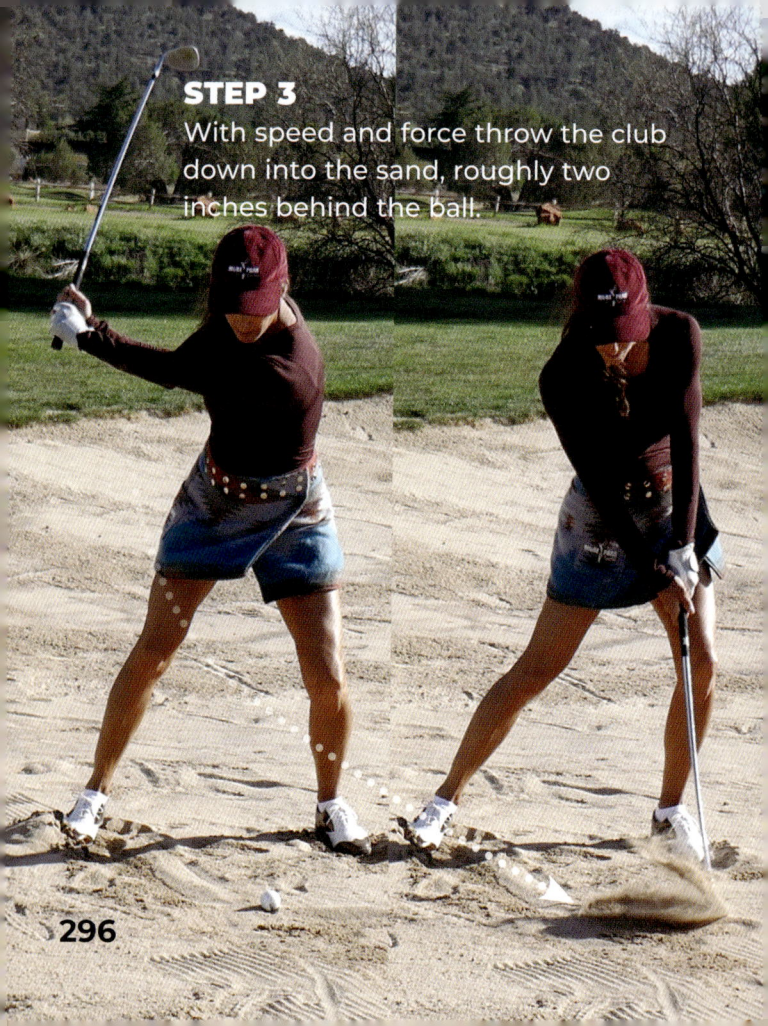

STEP 3

With speed and force throw the club down into the sand, roughly two inches behind the ball.

The sand takes the ball out.

STEP 4
Finish with the upper body facing the target and both feet fairly flat.

NO

Be your best coach. Assess your finish.

YES

"How much sand should I take?

300

Enter the sand two inches behind the ball. The ball hitches a ride on the magic carpet made of sand.

Long Greenside Bunker

STEP 1

Club selection is key. A sand wedge is not the best choice for this long carry out of the bunker. A pitching wedge or gap wedge are better choices.

STEP 2

Play a slightly open clubface with a narrow stance and ball centered. Stand tall to promote less sand contact.

STEP 3
Swing through with speed (fast arms) to ensure enough carry to the green.

Place more weight on the lead side and keep it there through the swing.

This shot requires a longer carry than the basic bunker shot, so get to a fuller finish.

Downslope

STEP 1

Mirror your body lines with the slope. Play the ball ahead of center. If a steep down slope, play it center. Place more weight on lead leg and keep it there through the swing.

STEP 2

Throw the club down into the sand a couple of inches behind ball.

307

Upslope

STEP 1
Mirror your body lines with the slope. Place more weight on the trail leg. Play the ball ahead of center.

STEP 2
Pivot the chest, as you hinge the club, while keeping the hands low.

STEP 3
Swing up the slope, keeping your body back to allow the club to swing up the slope through the sand.

Firm Sand or Buried Lie

An open face can literally bounce off the hard surface, so play a square face.

This is a plugged lie. Also referred to as a buried lie or fried egg.

STEP 1

Place more weight on lead leg. Keep it there through the swing. There is NO weight shift back. Play the ball ahead of center.

square face 311

STEP 2

Turn and hinge the club. Maintain the weight on lead side throughout the swing.

STEP 3

Throw the club vertically down into the sand. The finish is low with hands and club.

Close to the Edge

STEP 1
With a square face (SW or PW), keep the weight on your lead side as you rotate the chest and hinge the club.

STEP 2

Throw the club with force down into the sand, roughly two inches behind the ball. It should pop up and out.

the lip

HOW TO PLAY A
Fairway Bunker

Assess the lip and get a yardage.

STEP 1
How far is your ball from the lip? Is there is an opportunity to get it on the green.

STEP 2

I am using my 7-iron. Square the face and stand taller to promote a clean strike with minimal sand.

319

STEP 3
During the downswing stay in your posture, as you keep the legs more passive.

STEP 4
Finish tall and balanced.

321

Notes

CHIPS & PITCHES *THE ESSENTIALS*

323

This is a 35-yard pitch shot.

difference between
Chip vs. Pitch

> *When should I chip versus pitch?*

Pitch shots have a longer carry (more airtime) than a chip shot.

326

Chip Shot

This is a 20-yard chip.

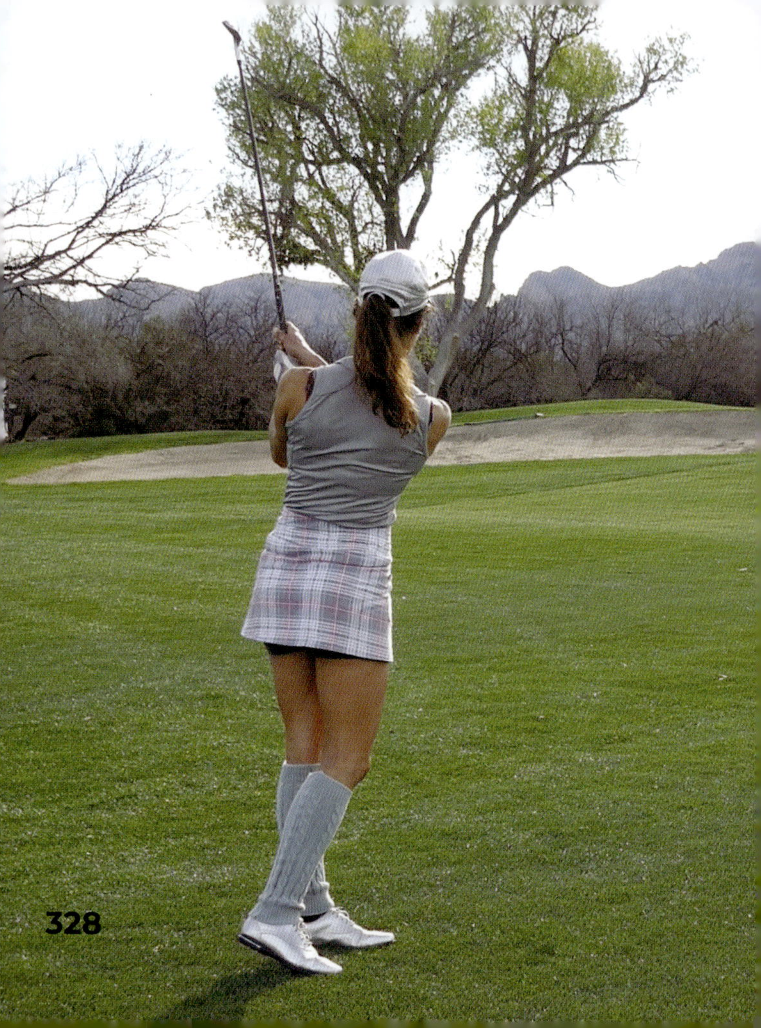

Pitch Shot

This is a pitch shot. I have a 45-yard carry to the green.

SIMPLIFY CHIPS WITH A
Capital Y

If you are new to chipping or struggle with solid contact, let's use the help of capital **Y**.

NO **YES**

Broken Y *Y intact*

331

As you pivot back and through, keep the capital Y intact.

Be sure to rotate through with the trail side, while maintaining your Y.

NO

The Y is broken due to a collapsed arm structure and lazy back side.

YES

The Y is intact. I rotated my back side through and maintained my arm structure!

386

"Which club should I use?

A sand wedge has more loft (more airtime). Land it closer to the hole.

A pitching wedge rolls out more (less loft). Land it half way to the hole.

An 8-iron rolls out the most. Land it just onto the green and let it roll to the hole.

338

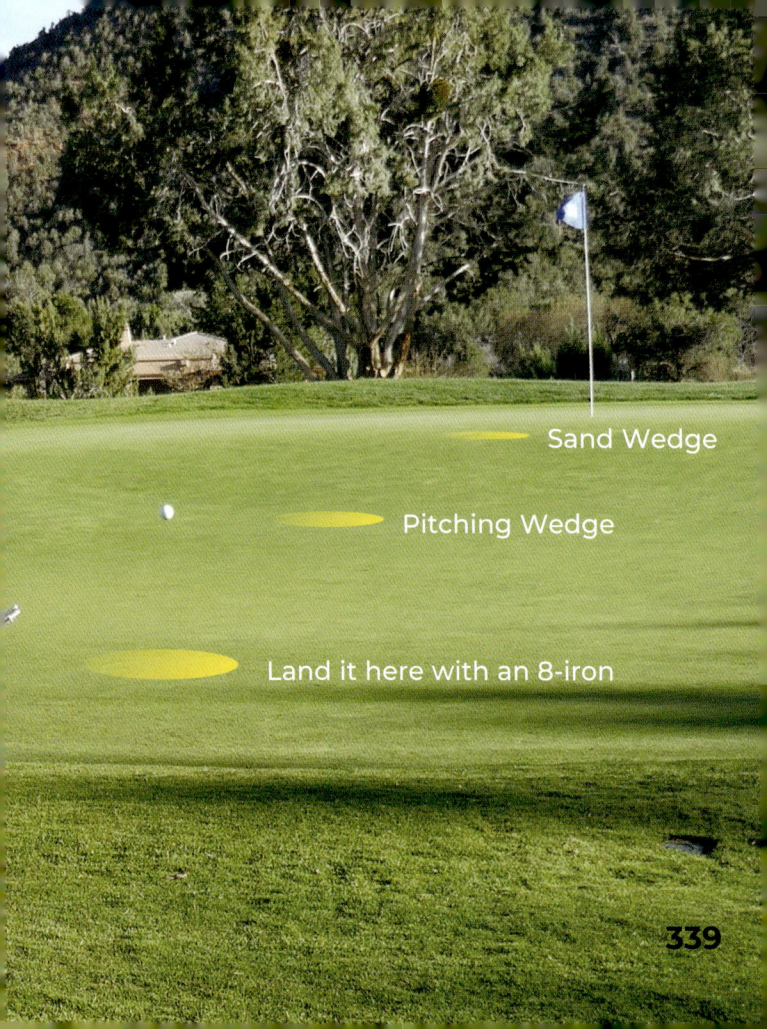

Sand Wedge

Pitching Wedge

Land it here with an 8-iron

FOCUS ON THE
Landing Spot

Players who focus on the flag land the ball there, and then discover that it rolls well past, leaving a challenging putt.

Instead, focus on a spot before the hole to allow for roll-out. The landing spot will depend on the club.

YES

NO

The landing spot is not the flag.

Dense Rough

STEP 1
Select a SW. Play the ball back of center with a slight open stance and clubface.

Create good hinge with the club.

342

STEP 2

This type of rough requires more hinge and a chop-down move. Drop the club into grass with a bit of force to pop the ball out.

STEP 2
Pivot the chest with the hands and club staying low.

STEP 1
Select a 7-, 8-, 9-iron or PW. To keep the ball low, play it back of center with more weight favoring your lead leg.

Low Runner

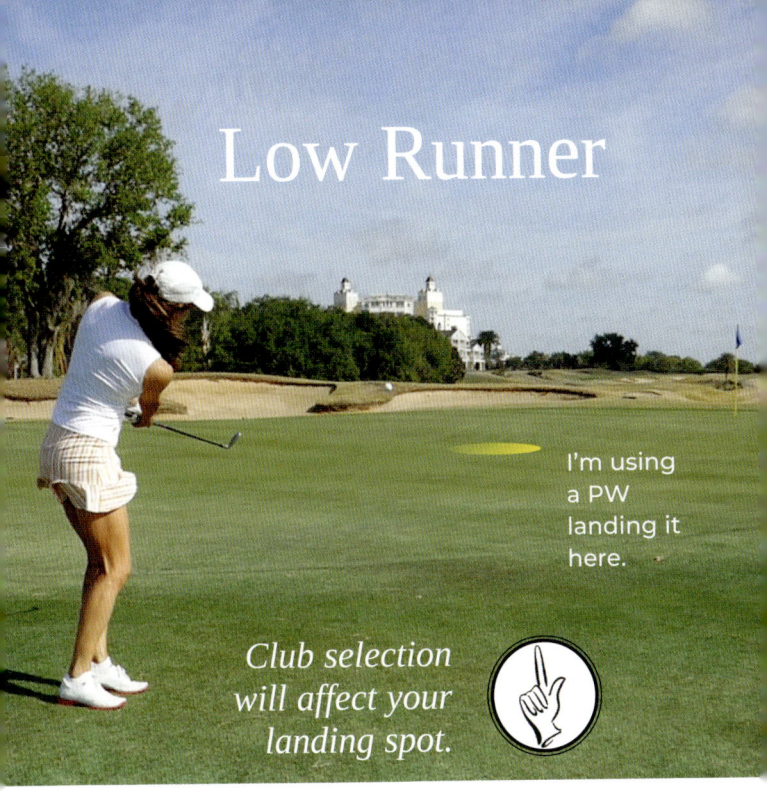

I'm using a PW landing it here.

Club selection will affect your landing spot.

STEP 3
To ensure a clean strike, hold your finish and stay in your posture well past impact.

Notes

ON THE GREEN TAKE A VACATION

347

> *I have too many 3-putts. Help!!*

The goal is to minimize 3-putts. If you have four to five a round currently, let's get that down to just two or three.

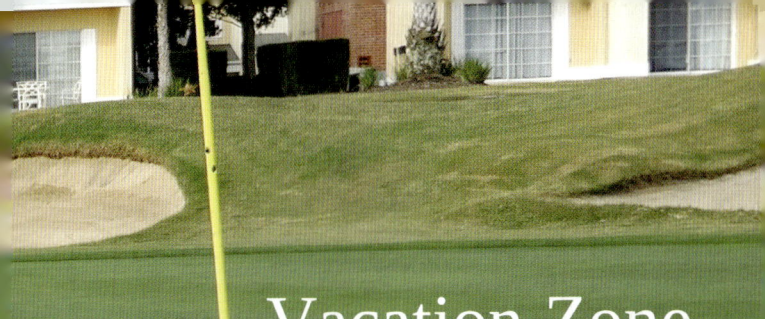

Vacation Zone

The goal with putting is to sink as many as possible on the first putt. That requires an approach or chip shot inside 10 feet. If outside 10 feet, the goal is rolling it close enough for an easy tap-in. I call this the vacation zone.

As the name implies, a putt inside the vacation zone means no stress. The range is inside 18 inches. It's so easy that you could tap it in playing a major PGA or LPGA event.

350

THIS IS DEFINITELY NOT

this is a vacation putt

THIS IS NOT

351

Equipment

Fit your putter around your putting style and posture.

In my camps and lessons, I see this way too often: Players are working their posture around their putter! Putting represents more that 50 percent of all your strokes during a round, yet few take the time to get fitted.

As with all clubs, the angle of a putter's shaft relative to the ground cannot exceed 80° when the club is in the address position. Most putters have a 70° lie angle. This is why the putting stroke has to swing on an arc (not straight back and straight through).

Clubfitter fits:
- Length
- Lie
- Loft
- Shaft Offset
- Head Style
- Grip Size

353

Players who work their posture around the putter are oftentimes too close or too far away from the ball. This will affect how you see the line, as well as direction.

YES

Drop the Ball

Check your distance from the ball. Drop a ball from your eye line. It should drop just inside or on the target line.

355

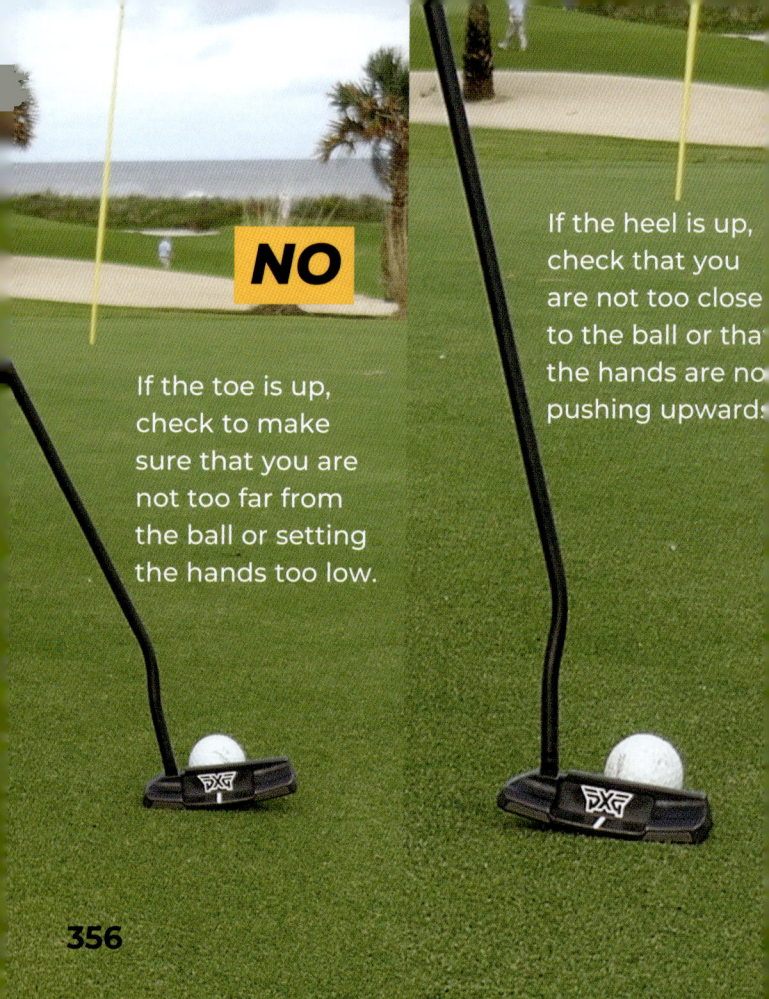

NO

If the toe is up, check to make sure that you are not too far from the ball or setting the hands too low.

If the heel is up, check that you are not too close to the ball or that the hands are not pushing upward.

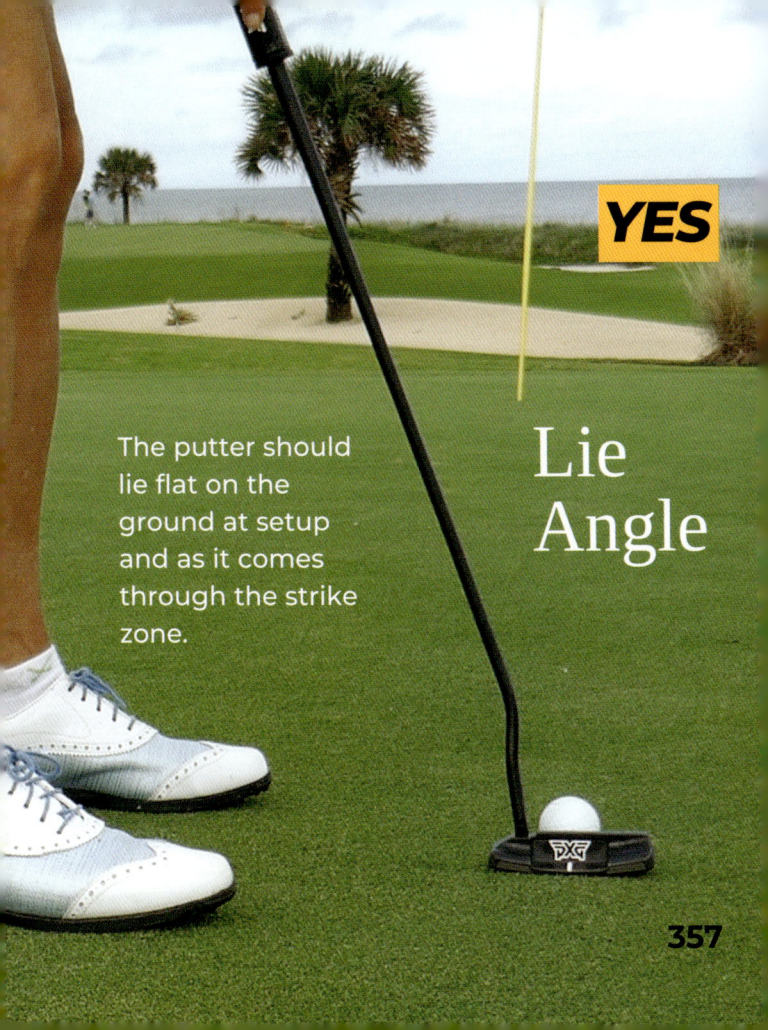

YES

Lie Angle

The putter should lie flat on the ground at setup and as it comes through the strike zone.

Reading the Green

Get down low and pay attention to breaks near the hole.

Confirm that this is the high side.

End here back at ball

START HERE

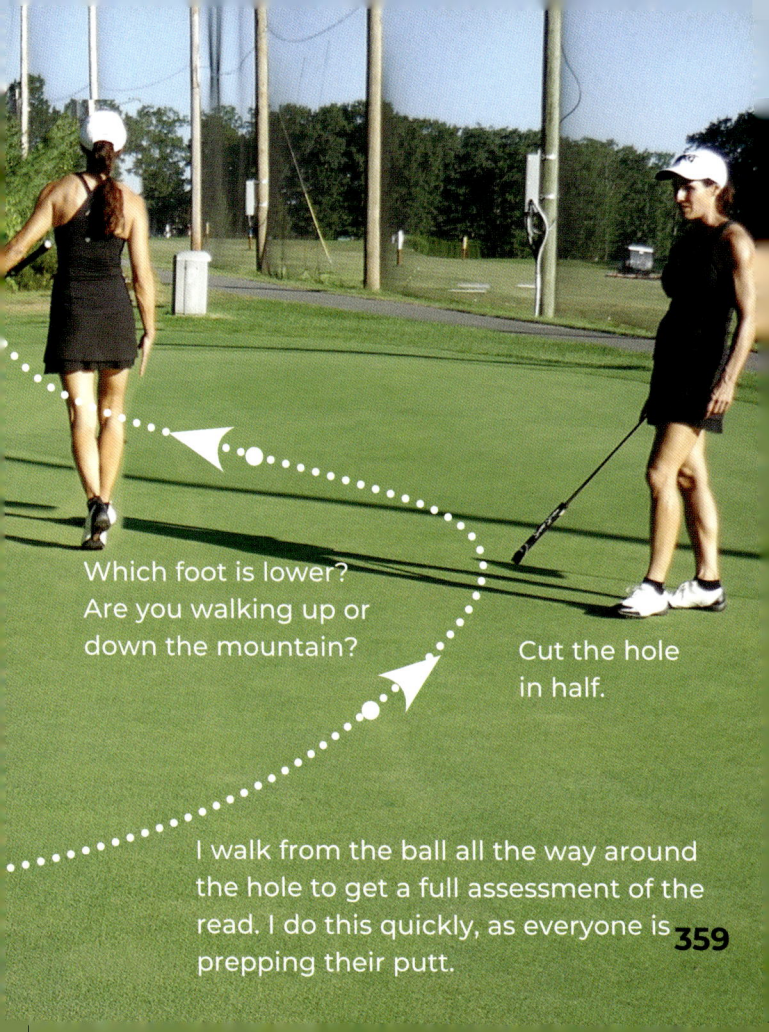

Which foot is lower? Are you walking up or down the mountain?

Cut the hole in half.

I walk from the ball all the way around the hole to get a full assessment of the read. I do this quickly, as everyone is prepping their putt.

Alignment

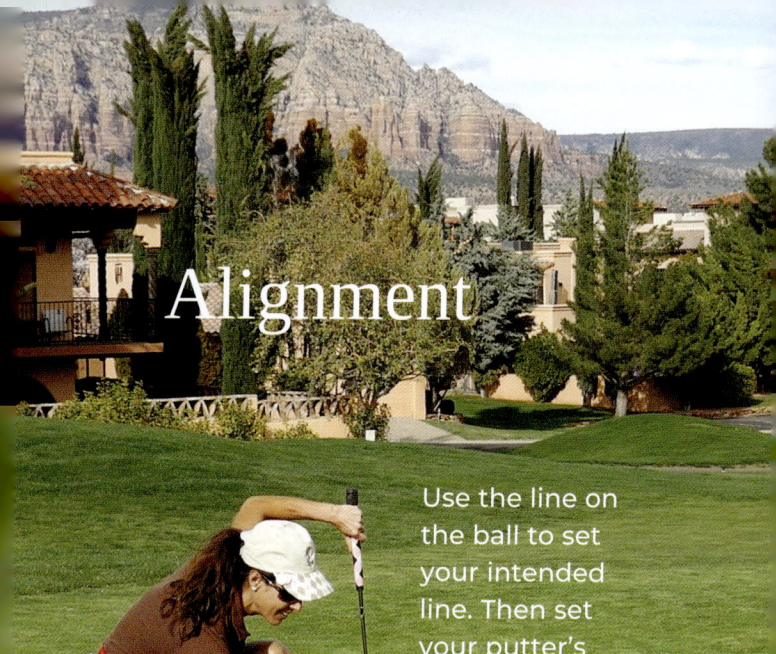

Use the line on the ball to set your intended line. Then set your putter's line on the ball line for an easy alignment process on the green.

360

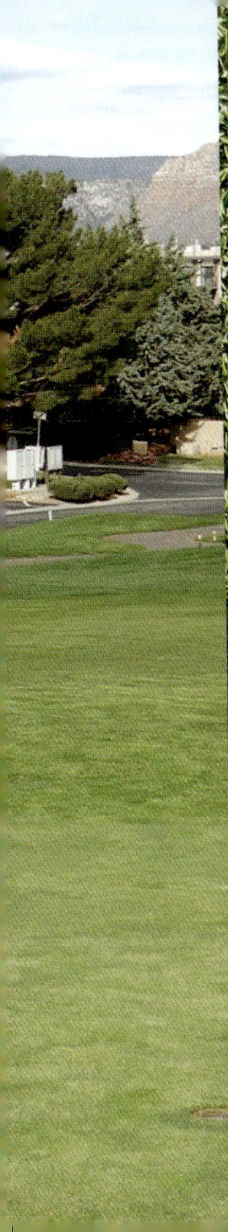

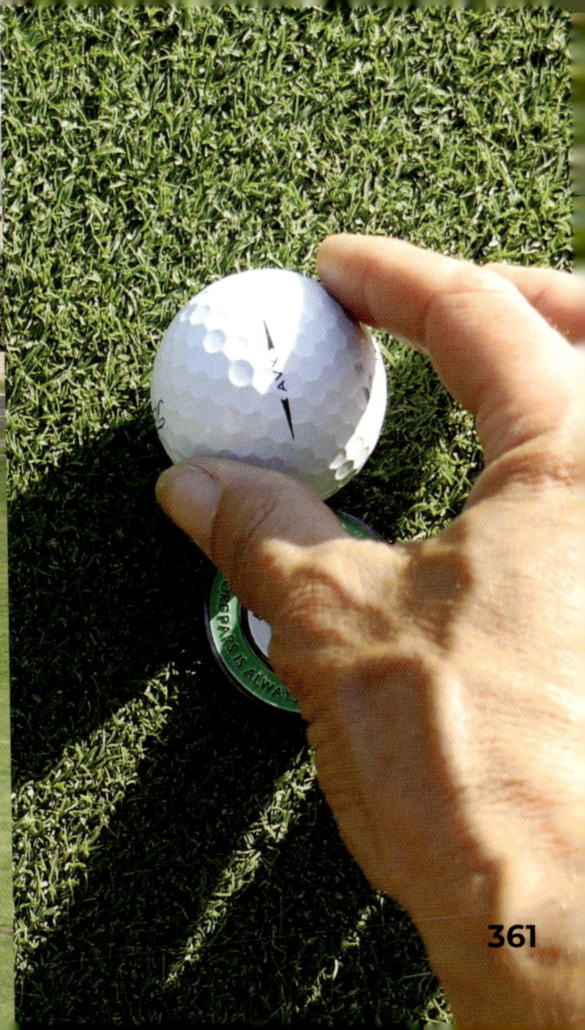

Do you take your regular grip with your putter?

YES

In the palms

In the fingers invites the wrist to come out to play.

NO

YES

In the palm creates a stable face with minimal wrist play.

365

Solid Setup

- Slightly outside hip-width stance or wider to promote solid legs

- Upper arms connected to torso with elbows facing in toward body

- Ball positioned center to just ahead of center

Amount of forward bend will be determined based on the length of putter and your preference. *Do you prefer a taller setup or more forward bend?*

Pressure points over the ankle

367

Solid Stroke

- Stable legs and a quiet head

- Keep arms connected to torso

- Shoulders work around spine

- Backstroke dictates length

Hold finish and head well past the putt to ensure solid contact. **369**

CONSISTENT

Speed
Control

Many players change the energy they give to a putt.

For example, with a longer putt, they'll strike it harder. For shorter putts, they'll take the foot off the gas. The problem with this scenario: it messes with physics, as the pendulum stroke likes to accelerate at the bottom of the arc. Instead, control the length of the putt with the length of the backstroke.

Control the length of the putt with the length of the backstroke. In general, players take too big of a backstroke.

longer putt   shorter putt

Keep the same energy when you strike the putt. Let the follow-through be fluid.

NO

Stroke Culprits
The Recoil

The recoil is when the player pulls the putter back quickly after the strike. This typically happens if there is tension in the stroke, doubt in the mind, or a forceful energy at impact.

*Players who **recoil**, struggle with distance and direction.*

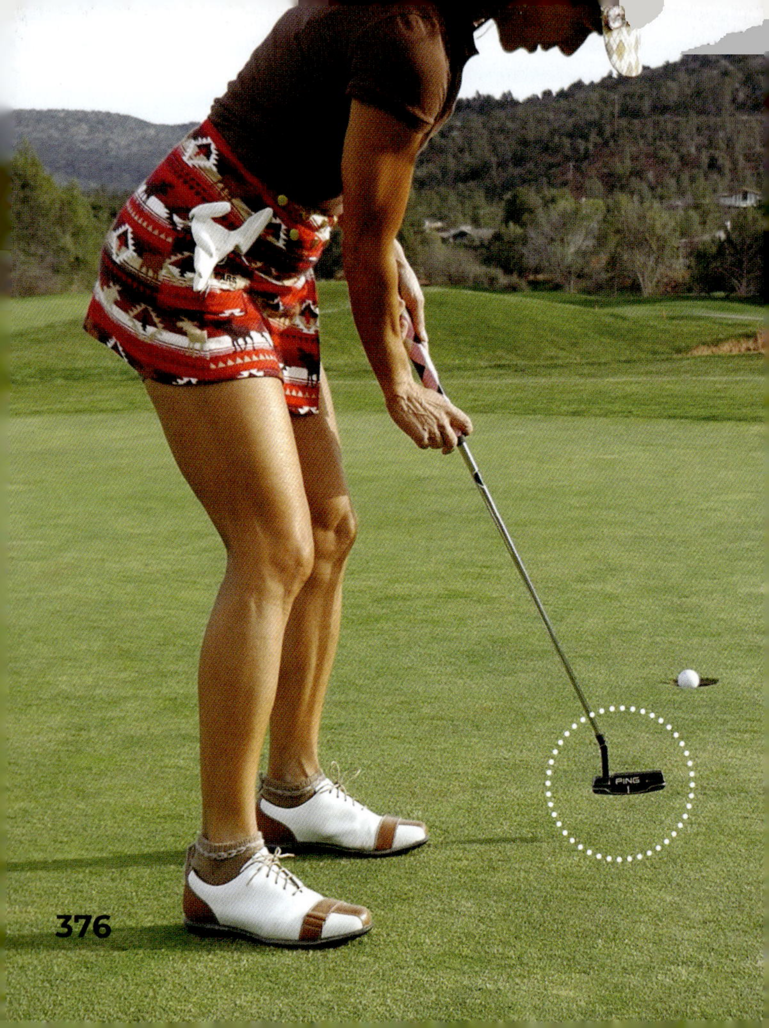
PING

Hold your finish!

YES

To eliminate the recoil, hold the finish for every putt. This smooths out your overall tempo and creates a stable putter face.

NO

Rockin' the Baby

I call this the *rockin' the baby* stroke, where the arms are working independently of the torso, creating an unstable putter face.

A popular culprit

If the arms are running the show, the putterface becomes unstable.

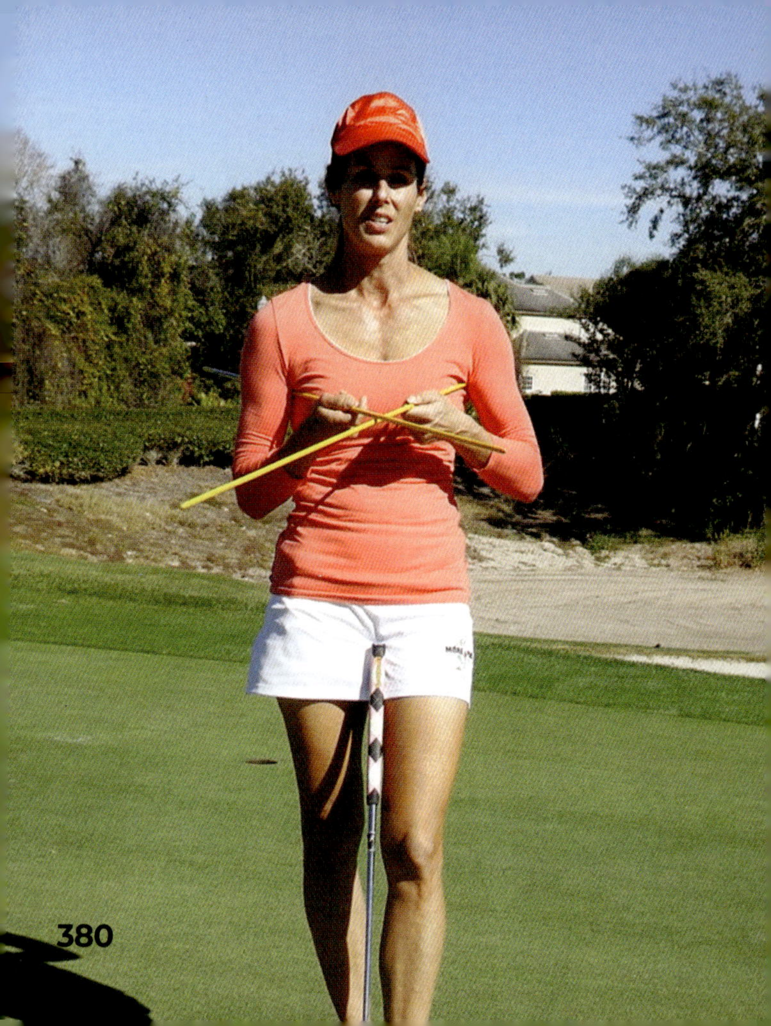

Shafts to Feel Connection

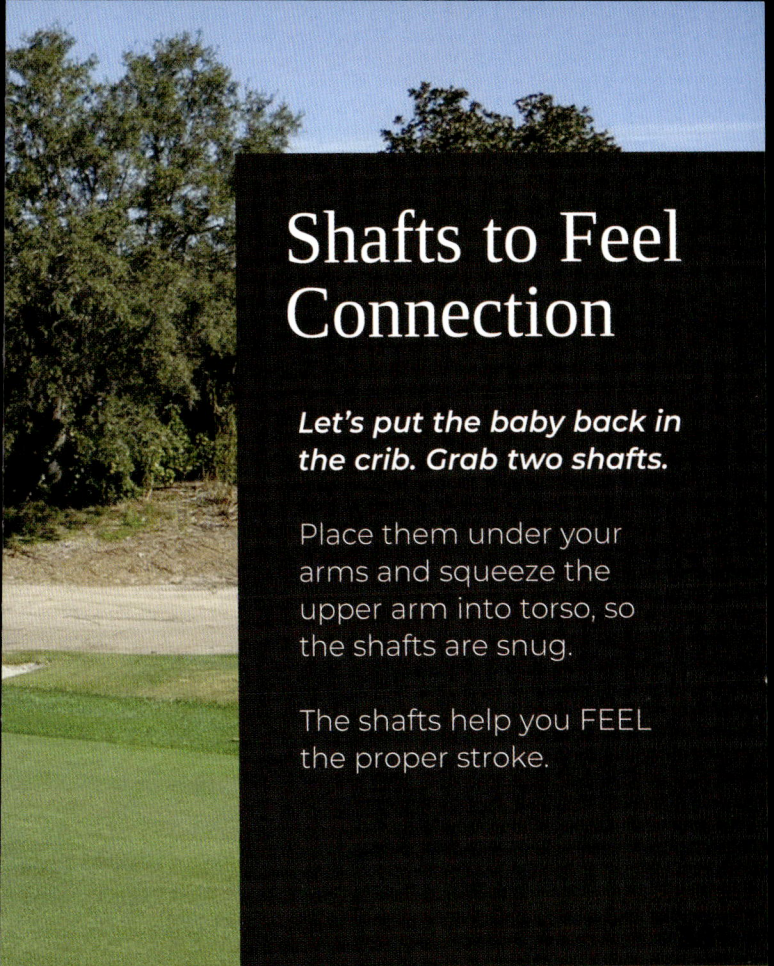

Let's put the baby back in the crib. Grab two shafts.

Place them under your arms and squeeze the upper arm into torso, so the shafts are snug.

The shafts help you FEEL the proper stroke.

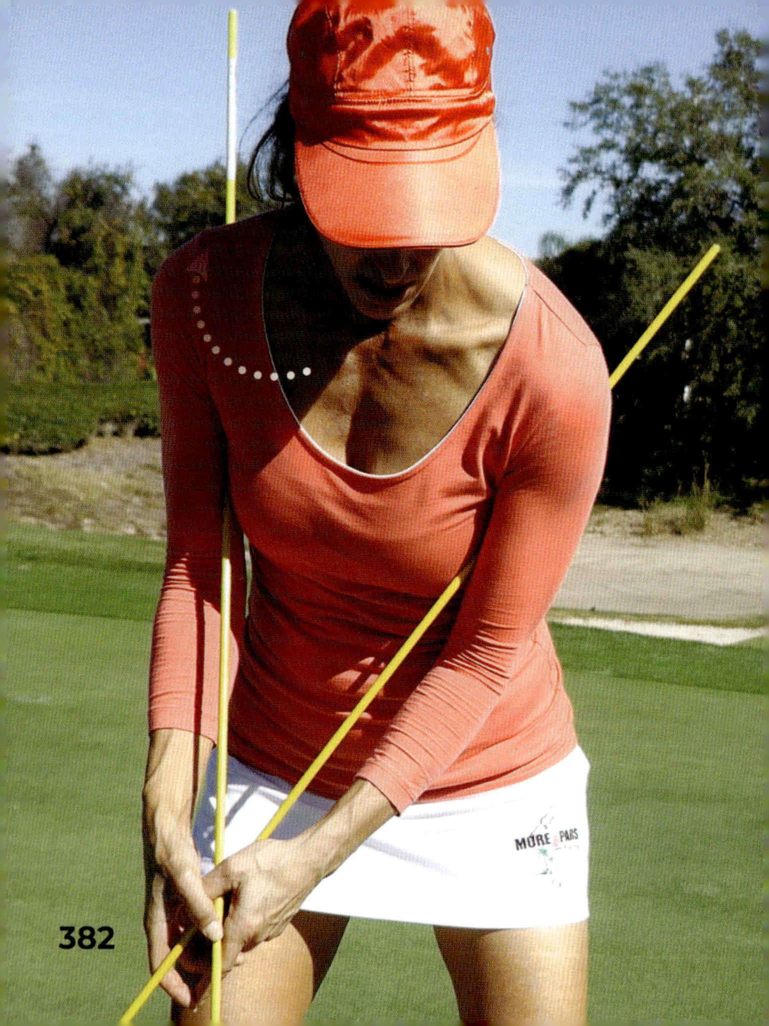
MORE PARS

Make a smooth, perpetual back and forth stroke. It should feel easy and fluid.

Download a metronome app or get the BlastGolf App. Both help you to discover your signature rhythm.

Groove Tempo

If your tempo changes on every putt, how can you be consistent?

Get consistent on the green with a consistent tempo. Some players prefer a 1-to-1 count, while others prefer a slower-paced backstroke (3-to-1 count). ***The key is to make sure that each stroke, regardless of length, has the same tempo ratio.***

AIM HERE

Aim vs. Apex

Every putt is a straight line until it begins its fall toward the hole.

The key is to find that point (apex) and aim higher. That is the aim point, not the apex. If you aim at the apex, you'll miss on the low side.

Groove Short Putts

STEP 1
Place a tee lightly on the back edge of the cup. It represents the line of the putt.

STEP 2
Strike the back of the cup in line with the tee.

Long & Downhill

IF SLOWER GREENS

IF FASTER GREENS

If the greens are running fast, visualize a hole closer than the actual. If running on the slow side, visualize a hole beyond to get it close.